UNLOCK

LISTENING & SPEAKING SKILLS

3

Sabina Ostrowska

D1558396

CAMBRIDGE
UNIVERSITY PRESS

University Printing House, Cambridge CB2 8BS, United Kingdom

Cambridge University Press is part of the University of Cambridge.

It furthers the University's mission by disseminating knowledge in the pursuit of education, learning and research at the highest international levels of excellence.

www.cambridge.org
Information on this title: www.cambridge.org/9781107687288

First published 2014

Printed in China by Golden Cup Printing Co. Ltd

A catalogue record for this publication is available from the British Library

ISBN 978-1-107-68728-8 Listening and Speaking 3 Student's Book with Online Workbook
ISBN 978-1-107-68154-5 Listening and Speaking 3 Teacher's Book with DVD
ISBN 978-1-107-61526-7 Reading and Writing 3 Student's Book with Online Workbook
ISBN 978-1-107-61404-8 Reading and Writing 3 Teacher's Book with DVD

Additional resources for this publication at www.cambridge.org/unlock

CONTENTS

MAP OF THE BOOK

UNIT	VIDEO	LISTENING	VOCABULARY	
1 ANIMALS LISTENING 1: A podcast with a veterinary student (Biology) LISTENING 2: A debate about using animals for work (Politics)	Wildlife conservation	*Key listening skill*: Taking notes Understanding key vocabulary Using visuals to predict content Listening for detail Predicting content Listening for main ideas Listening for opinion *Pronunciation for listening*: Intonation of lists	Word families (e.g. *analysis, analyze, analytical, analytically*)	
2 CUSTOMS AND TRADITIONS LISTENING 1: A radio programme about changing customs in the modern world (Sociology) LISTENING 2: A discussion about new social-networking habits (Culture)	Japan: customs and traditions	*Key listening skill*: Identifying cause and effect Understanding key vocabulary Predicting content Listening for main ideas Listening for detail Using your knowledge *Pronunciation for listening*: Connected speech: final /t/ and /d/	Suffixes (e.g. *-al, -ise, -able, -ful, -less*)	
3 HISTORY LISTENING 1: A discussion about major historical finds (History) LISTENING 2: A lecture about Sultan Mehmed II (History)	The desert mummies of Peru	*Key listening skill*: Understanding key vocabulary Using your knowledge Listening for main ideas Listening for detail Listening for text organisation features *Pronunciation for listening*: Connected speech: weak forms	Synonyms (e.g. *soldiers, warriors, find, discover*)	
4 TRANSPORT LISTENING 1: A radio programme about fear of flying (Psychology) LISTENING 2: A focus-group discussion about cycling (Sociology)	How to make a BMW	*Key listening skill*: Identifying rhetorical questions Understanding key vocabulary Using your knowledge Listening for main ideas Listening for detail Taking notes Listening for text organisation features *Pronunciation for listening*: Word stress	Talking about achievement (e.g. *challenge, goal, attitude*)	
5 ENVIRONMENT LISTENING 1: A lecture about agriculture (Ecology) LISTENING 2: A debate about nuclear energy (politics)	Sleeping giants: Russia's volcanoes	*Key listening skill*: Understanding explanations Understanding key vocabulary Predicting content from visuals Listening for main ideas Listening for detail Listening for text organisation features Listening for counter-arguments *Pronunciation for listening*: Connected speech: linking sounds	Negative prefixes (e.g. *un-, in-, im-*)	

GRAMMAR	CRITICAL THINKING	SPEAKING
Modals for obligation and suggestions (*have to, have got to, should, need to, must, ought to*) Contrasting ideas (e.g. *but, yet, however*)	Giving examples to support an opinion	***Preparation for speaking***: Preparing an opening statement for a debate, using signposting language to help the audience ***Pronunciation for speaking:*** Introducing examples ***Speaking task:*** Give an opening statement in a debate: Using animals for entertainment should be banned.
Dependent prepositions	Ideas maps Identifying advantages and disadvantages	***Preparation for speaking***: Taking turns in a discussion Using adverbs for emphasis ***Pronunciation for speaking:*** Phrases to emphasize agreeing and disagreeing (e.g. *I strongly believe that ... , I completely disagree that ...*) ***Speaking task:*** How has modern technology changed the way we interact with each other? What are the positive and negative aspects of this influence?
Relative clauses	Distinguishing between facts and opinions	***Preparation for speaking***: Talking about past events ***Pronunciation for speaking:*** Past tense regular verbs /t/ /d/ /id/ Talking about time ***Speaking task:*** Give a presentation about a famous historical figure or a historical event
Comparing things (e.g. *by far, considerably more, definitely more*)	Evaluating and proposing ideas	***Preparation for speaking***: Expanding ideas and giving examples of personal experiences ***Speaking task:*** Take part in a group discussion about using your mobile phone while walking.
Modals to express opinions (e.g. *might be, could, may*)	Giving counter-arguments	***Preparation for speaking***: Linking ideas Talking about advantages and disadvantages ***Speaking task:*** You are a member of a city council that has to decide how to develop a large piece of land. Argue for or against building a new shopping centre.

UNIT	VIDEO	LISTENING	VOCABULARY	
6 HEALTH AND FITNESS LISTENING 1: A radio programme about healthy lifestyles (Fitness) LISTENING 2: Health advertisements (Health)	Training for a triathlon: the ultimate event	*Key listening skill*: Identifying attitude Understanding key vocabulary Using your knowledge Listening for main ideas Referring to common knowledge Listening for detail *Pronunciation for listening*: Intonation: expressing attitudes	Phrasal verbs (e.g. *go out, bring up, take up*)	
7 DISCOVERY AND INVENTION LISTENING 1: A talk about inventions (Discovery) LISTENING 2: A lecture about mobile phone apps (Invention)	Engineering a ski resort in the desert	*Key listening skill*: Understanding lecture organisation Understanding key vocabulary Using your knowledge Listening for main ideas Listening for detail Referring to earlier ideas Taking notes Listening for text organisation features *Pronunciation for listening*: Weak forms and strong forms	Phrases with *make* (e.g. *make a discovery, make sure, make a difference*)	
8 FASHION LISTENING 1: A discussion about clothes (Fashion) LISTENING 2: Interview with a designer (Business)	From function to fashion	*Key listening skill*: Listening for detail Understanding key vocabulary Using visuals to predict content Listening for main ideas Using your knowledge *Pronunciation for listening*: Vowel elision	Idioms and fixed expressions (e.g. *I see what you mean, give me a hand, at long last*)	
9 ECONOMICS LISTENING 1: A radio programme about millionaire lifestyles (Sociology) LISTENING 2: A discussion about whether college students should be paid for good grades (Economics)	Economic migration: the Chinese dream	*Key listening skill*: Understanding key vocabulary Using your knowledge to predict content Listening for main ideas Listening for detail Referring to research Identifying opposing points of view *Pronunciation for listening*: Silent letters	Collocations with *pay, save* and *money* (e.g. *pay in cash, save energy, borrow money*)	
10 THE BRAIN LISTENING 1: An interview about what makes a genius (Psychology) LISTENING 2: A formal conversation about brain health (Health)	The placebo effect	*Key listening skill*: Understanding paraphrase Using your knowledge to predict content Listening for main ideas Listening for detail *Pronunciation for listening*: Intonation in questions	Collocations with *mind* (e.g. *mind your own business, never mind, speak your mind*	

GRAMMAR	CRITICAL THINKING	SPEAKING
Talking about preferences (e.g. *I'd rather, I'd prefer*)	Analyzing persuasive language in advertisements	**Preparation for speaking**: Planning to persuade someone Using imperatives Using adjectives **Speaking task**: Create an advertisement for an alternative treatment.
Passive forms	Researching a topic using *Wh-* questions and ideas maps	**Preparation for speaking**: Outlining a topic Organizing ideas Explaining how something is used **Speaking task**: Give a presentation about an invention or discovery that has changed our lives.
Talking about the future	Raising and discussing alternative points of view	**Preparation for speaking**: Asking for opinions and checking information Focusing on information that follows **Speaking task**: Interview people to find out attitudes towards uniforms and dress codes.
Conditional sentences	Identifying and explaining opinions for and against an idea	**Preparation for speaking**: Using *-ing* verb forms to talk about actions Asking someone to explain in more detail **Speaking task**: Debate whether young people should have credit cards.
Modal verbs for giving advice (*If I were you, I would ...; You should ...; You ought to ...*)	Analysing and applying the idea of multiple intelligences	**Preparation for speaking**: Asking for and giving advice Using *-ing* verb forms to talk about actions **Speaking task**: Ask for and give advice on how to study effectively and what type of courses to consider.

UNL⊘CK UNIT STRUCTURE

The units in *Unlock Listening and Speaking Skills* are carefully scaffolded so that students build the skills and language they need throughout the unit in order to produce a successful Speaking task.

UNLOCK YOUR KNOWLEDGE	Encourages discussion around the theme of the unit with inspiration from interesting questions and striking visuals.

WATCH AND LISTEN	Features an engaging and motivating *Discovery Education™* video which generates interest in the topic.

LISTENING 1	Provides information about the topic and practises pre-listening, while listening and post-listening skills. This section also includes a focus on a pronunciation feature which will further enhance listening comprehension.

LANGUAGE DEVELOPMENT	Practises the vocabulary and grammar from Listening 1 and pre-teaches the vocabulary and grammar from Listening 2.

LISTENING 2	Provides a different angle on the topic and serves as a model for the speaking task.

CRITICAL THINKING	Contains brainstorming, categorising, evaluative and analytical tasks as preparation for the speaking task.

PREPARATION FOR SPEAKING / SPEAKING SKILLS	Presents and practises functional language, pronunciation and speaking strategies for the speaking task.

SPEAKING TASK	Uses the skills and strategies learnt over the course of the unit to produce a presentational or interactional speaking task.

OBJECTIVES REVIEW	Allows learners to assess how well they have mastered the skills covered in the unit.

WORDLIST	Includes the key vocabulary from the unit.

This is the unit's main learning objective. It gives learners the opportunity to use all the language and skills they have learnt in the unit.

UNLOCK MOTIVATION

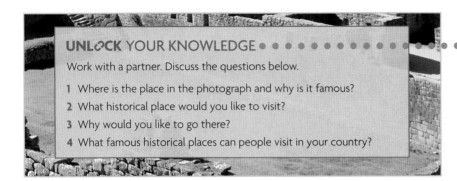

UNLOCK YOUR KNOWLEDGE • • • • • • • • • • • • • • • • •

Work with a partner. Discuss the questions below.

1 Where is the place in the photograph and why is it famous?
2 What historical place would you like to visit?
3 Why would you like to go there?
4 What famous historical places can people visit in your country?

PERSONALIZE

Unlock encourages students to bring their own knowledge, experiences and opinions to the topics. This **motivates** students to relate the topics to their own contexts.

DISCOVERY EDUCATION™ VIDEO

Thought-provoking videos from *Discovery Education™* are included in every unit throughout the course to introduce topics, promote discussion and motivate learners. The videos provide a new angle on a wide range of academic subjects.

❝ The video was excellent! It helped with raising students' interest in the topic. It was well-structured and the language level was appropriate.

Maria Agata Szczerbik,
United Arab Emirates University,
Al-Ain, UAE ❞

UNL⌀CK CRITICAL THINKING

> " […] with different styles of visual aids such as mind maps, grids, tables and pictures, this [critical thinking] section [provides] very crucial tools that can encourage learners to develop their speaking skills.
>
> Dr. Panidnad Chulerk, Rangit University, Thailand "

BLOOM'S TAXONOMY

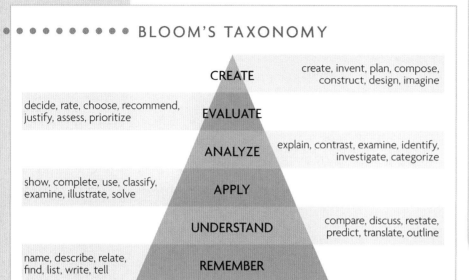

CREATE — create, invent, plan, compose, construct, design, imagine

EVALUATE — decide, rate, choose, recommend, justify, assess, prioritize

ANALYZE — explain, contrast, examine, identify, investigate, categorize

APPLY — show, complete, use, classify, examine, illustrate, solve

UNDERSTAND — compare, discuss, restate, predict, translate, outline

REMEMBER — name, describe, relate, find, list, write, tell

BLOOM'S TAXONOMY

The Critical thinking sections in *Unlock* are based on Benjamin Bloom's classification of learning objectives. This ensures learners develop their **lower-** and **higher-order thinking skills**, ranging from demonstrating **knowledge** and **understanding** to in-depth **evaluation**.
The margin headings in the Critical thinking sections highlight the exercises which develop Bloom's concepts.

LEARN TO THINK

Learners engage in **evaluative** and **analytical tasks** that are designed to ensure they do all of the thinking and information-gathering required for the end-of-unit speaking task.

CRITICAL THINKING

At the end of this unit you are going to do the speaking task below.

> How has modern technology changed the way we interact with each other? What are the positive and negative aspects of this influence?

UNDERSTAND

1 Look at the ideas map. What is the main focus?

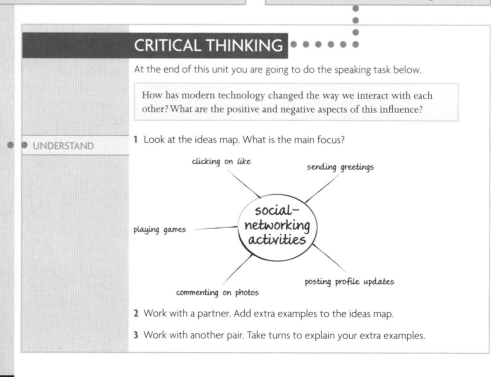

clicking on like
sending greetings
playing games
social-networking activities
commenting on photos
posting profile updates

2 Work with a partner. Add extra examples to the ideas map.

3 Work with another pair. Take turns to explain your extra examples.

UNL⌀CK RESEARCH

THE CAMBRIDGE LEARNER CORPUS ◉

The **Cambridge Learner Corpus** is a bank of official Cambridge English exam papers. Our exclusive access means we can use the corpus to carry out unique research and identify the most common errors that learners make. That information is used to ensure the *Unlock* syllabus teaches the most **relevant language**.

THE WORDS YOU NEED

Language Development sections provide vocabulary and grammar-building tasks that are further practised in the ⌀ **UNL⌀CK ONLINE** Workbook. The glossary provides definitions and pronunciation, and the end-of-unit wordlists provide useful summaries of key vocabulary.

◉ LANGUAGE DEVELOPMENT ⌀ UNL⌀CK ONLINE

Word families
You can develop your academic vocabulary by working on word families. When you record a new word in your notebook, make sure to write down any other forms from its word family.

1   Complete the table below. Sometimes there is more than one possible answer. Use a dictionary to help you.

noun	verb	adjective	adverb

PRONUNCIATION FOR LISTENING ⌀ UNL⌀CK ONLINE

Connected speech: weak forms
When we speak fluently, some words are not usually pronounced in a strong or clear way. These are usually auxiliary verbs (*has, was, do*, etc.), modals (*would, can*, etc.), prepositions (*to, for*, etc.) and other small words (*and, you*, etc.).

When small words are not pronounced clearly, we call this a 'weak form'. These words are pronounced with a /ə/ sound.

4   ◀)) 3.2 Listen to extracts from the discussion. Notice the pronunciation of the highlighted words.

1   Has the professor sent us the list of possible topics to choose from?
2   OK, we can do that.
3   Some of them are human and some are animals.

ACADEMIC LANGUAGE

Unique research using the **Cambridge English Corpus** has been carried out into academic language, in order to provide learners with relevant, academic vocabulary from the start (CEFR A1 and above). This addresses a gap in current academic vocabulary mapping and ensures learners are presented with carefully selected words which they will find essential during their studies.

PRONUNCIATION FOR LISTENING

This unique feature of *Unlock* focuses on aspects of pronunciation which may inhibit listening comprehension. This means that learners are primed to understand detail and nuance while listening.

> ❝ The language development is clear and the strong lexical focus is positive as learners feel they make more progress when they learn more vocabulary. ❞
>
> Colleen Wackrow,
> Princess Nourah Bint Abdulrahman University, Al-Riyadh, Kingdom of Saudi Arabia

UNLOCK SOLUTIONS

FLEXIBLE

Unlock is available in a range of print and digital components, so teachers can mix and match according to their requirements.

UNLOCK ONLINE WORKBOOKS

The **UNLOCK ONLINE** Workbooks are accessed via activation codes packaged with the Student's Books. These **easy-to-use** workbooks provide interactive exercises, games, tasks, and further practice of the language and skills from the Student's Books in the Cambridge LMS, an engaging and modern learning environment.

CAMBRIDGE LEARNING MANAGEMENT SYSTEM (LMS)

The Cambridge LMS provides teachers with the ability to track learner progress and save valuable time thanks to automated marking functionality. Blogs, forums and other tools are also available to facilitate communication between students and teachers.

UNLOCK EBOOKS

The *Unlock* Student's Books and Teacher's Books are also available as interactive eBooks. With answers and *Discovery Education*™ videos embedded, the eBooks provide a great alternative to the printed materials.

COURSE COMPONENTS

- Each level of *Unlock* consists of two Student's Books: **Reading & Writing** and **Listening & Speaking** and an accompanying Teacher's Book for each. Online Workbooks are packaged with each Student's Book.
- Complete course audio is available to download from www.cambridge.org/unlock
- Look out for the **UNLOCK ONLINE** symbols in the Student's Books which indicate that additional practice of that skill or language area is available in the Online Workbook.
- Every *Unlock* Student's Book is delivered both in print format and as an interactive **eBook for tablet devices**.
- The *Unlock* Teacher's Books contain additional speaking tasks, tests, teaching tips and research projects for students.
- *Presentation Plus* **software for interactive whiteboards** is available for all Student's Books.

LISTENING AND SPEAKING

Student's Book and Online Workbook Pack*	978-1-107-67810-1	978-1-107-68232-0	978-1-107-68728-8	978-1-107-63461-9
Teacher's Book with DVD*	978-1-107-66211-7	978-1-107-64280-5	978-1-107-68154-5	978-1-107-65052-7
Presentation Plus (interactive whiteboard software)	978-1-107-66424-1	978-1-107-69582-5	978-1-107-63543-2	978-1-107-64381-9

*eBooks available from **www.cambridge.org/unlock**

The complete course audio is available from
www.cambridge.org/unlock

READING AND WRITING

Student's Book and Online Workbook Pack*	978-1-107-61399-7	978-1-107-61400-0	978-1-107-61526-7	978-1-107-61525-0
Teacher's Book with DVD*	978-1-107-61401-7	978-1-107-61403-1	978-1-107-61404-8	978-1-107-61409-3
Presentation Plus (interactive whiteboard software)	978-1-107-63800-6	978-1-107-65605-5	978-1-107-67624-4	978-1-107-68245-0

*eBooks available from **www.cambridge.org/unlock**

LEARNING OBJECTIVES

Watch and listen	Watch and understand a video about a wildlife organization
Listening skills	Take notes
Speaking skills	Use signposting language; introduce examples; express general beliefs
Speaking task	Give an opening statement in a debate

UNLOCK YOUR KNOWLEDGE

Work with a partner. Discuss the questions below.

1 Look at the photo. What work are the dogs doing?
2 What other types of work can animals do?
3 Are animals used for work in your country?
  If yes, what work do they do?

WATCH AND LISTEN

PREPARING TO WATCH

UNDERSTANDING KEY VOCABULARY

1 Read the information below about an organization. What does the organization do?

> This animal organization focuses on **wildlife conservation**. They protect endangered species. In order to help wild animals, the organization sometimes has to **capture** and **relocate** them to a safer place. Catching a giraffe on the **savannah**, which is a huge area, can be difficult. It's easier to catch the animals when they are in a **herd**. The vets often have to **sedate** wild animals to calm them down before moving them.

2 Match the words in bold in Exercise 1 with the definitions below. Try to guess the meaning from the context.

1 _____ : a group of animals that live and eat together
2 _____ : to catch someone or something
3 _____ : the protection of animals, birds and plants
4 _____ : to make someone or something calm or go to sleep
5 _____ : a large area in a hot climate where very few trees grow
6 _____ : to move something to a new place

WHILE WATCHING

UNDERSTANDING MAIN IDEAS

3 ▶ Watch the video. Which animals are mentioned?

1 lions
2 tigers
3 rhinos
4 zebras

5 elephants
6 giraffes
7 gazelles
8 pandas

UNL🔒CK LISTENING AND SPEAKING SKILLS 3

4 ▶ Watch again. Choose the best caption (a, b or c) for each photograph on page 16.

Photo 1
a Many people live in South Africa.
b The South African savannah is a huge area of grassland.
c Springboks live in the savannah.

Photo 2
a South African vets travel huge distances.
b Every vet in South Africa is a pilot.
c The vet enjoys the flight.

Photo 3
a Giraffes like to live together.
b It takes an hour to find the herd.
c The herd needs to be relocated.

Photo 4
a The team is used to working with giraffes.
b The giraffe will be taken to a zoo.
c The giraffe will travel 800 kilometres to a new home.

5 ▶ Watch again. Write true (T) or false (F) next to the statements below.

UNDERSTANDING
DETAIL

1 This national park is in the east of the country.
2 It rains a lot in this area.
3 Jana Pretorius relocates 8,000 animals each month.
4 10% of South Africa is used for protecting wildlife.
5 The sedative could kill people.
6 Jana's team only travels by helicopter.
7 It takes Jana one day to find the herd.
8 The giraffe dies in the end.

DISCUSSION

6 Work with a partner. Discuss the questions below.

1 Would you like to work with wild animals? Why / Why not?
2 What are some advantages of Jana's job?
3 What are the disadvantages of her job?
4 What other jobs involve working with animals?

PREPARING TO LISTEN

1 You are going to listen to a programme about animals. Before you listen, read the extracts below. Match the words in bold to the definitions (a–j).

1 I help examine, diagnose and **treat** sick animals.
2 I help with the animals – clean them, **feed** them and **take care of** them.
3 At the veterinary school, we can choose between small animals like cats and dogs, or large animals like camels, horses, cows ... My **specialization** is small animals, like cats and dogs.
4 In the third year, we did more **lab** work. It was surprising how often **vets** need to analyze lab **results**.
5 We do get a lot of **emergencies**. The most common ones involve food poisoning or bites. Many pet owners don't realize that food which is **harmless** to humans can be dangerous to pets. For example, chocolate is **poisonous** to cats and dogs.

a give medical care to someone or something that is ill   *treat*
b laboratory – a room used for scientific tests
c to make sure something or someone is safe and looked after
d people whose job is to give medical care to animals
e to give food to a person or an animal
f very harmful and able to make you sick or kill you
g serious situations that need immediate attention
h a specific area of knowledge that you can study
i information that you get from an experiment or a test
j not dangerous

2 Read the advert on page 19 and choose the best answer to the questions below.

1 What kind of programme do you think it will be?
a a radio show
b the news
c a university podcast
2 Who do you think will be interviewed?
a a medical doctor
b a veterinary student
c a zoo director
3 What do you think will be the guest's attitude towards animals?
a She likes them a lot.
b She is afraid of them.
c She thinks they are difficult to love.

News from your university,
campus updates and interviews with
students and teachers.

Most recent episode
You have to love animals to do this job!

Click <u>here</u> to download. **(9MB)**

Subscribe
for free!

3 🔊**1.1** Listen to the first part of the programme and check.

PRONUNCIATION FOR LISTENING

Intonation of lists

The student in the programme is very interested in her subject and wants to help
the listeners understand it. She lists animals and activities to help explain her
ideas. We often make lists to give the listener examples of what we are talking
about. These lists have their own intonation patterns.

4 🔊**1.2** Listen to two extracts from the radio programme. Then circle the
correct rule about the intonation of lists.

1 We've always been surrounded by animals – like ...

  ↗   ↗ ↗   ↗   ↗
<u>cats</u>, <u>dogs</u>, <u>donkeys</u>, <u>goats</u>, <u>horses</u> ...

• The speaker pauses between each animal in the list, and stresses each
  word. In this example, the last word in the list has rising intonation. The
  speaker thinks this *is / is not* a complete list.

2 Well, my job was to help with the animals ...

  ↗   ↗   ↘
<u>clean</u> them, <u>feed</u> them and take <u>care</u> of them.

• The speaker pauses between each activity in the list. In this example,
  the *first / last* activity has falling intonation. The speaker
  wants / doesn't want to add more examples, and the list is
  finished / not finished.

5 🔊**1.2** Listen again. Practise saying the sentences.

WHILE LISTENING

Taking notes

Taking notes is an important skill when we listen to long texts. Everyone has their own note-taking style, so choose a style you are comfortable with.

UNLOCK
ONLINE

6 🔊**1.3** Listen to the next part of the programme and complete the notes.

Specializations	Emergencies
1 _____	• food poisoning, e.g. _____
2 _____	can poison cats & dogs
3 exotic animals	• _____
Vet studies	*Tips for vet sts.*
1st & 2nd yr. _____	• think about it _____
3rd yr. _____	• _____ e.g. animal shelter,
4th yr. _____	zoo, etc.

7 The notes in Exercise 6 include abbreviations. Match the abbreviations (1–5) to the meanings (a–e).

1 yr.	a and
2 e.g.	b students
3 sts.	c etcetera (= and so on)
4 etc.	d for example
5 &	e year

POST-LISTENING

8 Look at the sentences below. Guess the meaning of the words in bold.

1 I help examine, **diagnose** and treat sick animals.
  a wash
  b recognize an illness

2 And the last one is **exotic** animals – like snakes.
  a unusual or foreign
  b pets

3 It was an amazing experience and it **convinced** me to apply for veterinary school.
  a disagree
  b make someone decide something

4 Many pet owners don't **realize** that food which is harmless to humans can be dangerous to their pets.
  a believe
  b know or understand

DISCUSSION

9 Work in small groups and discuss the questions below.

1 Do you think it is important to look after animals? Why?
2 Do you think some animals are more important than others? Why / Why not?
3 What can people do to take better care of animals?

⊙ LANGUAGE DEVELOPMENT

WORD FAMILIES

Word families

You can develop your academic vocabulary by working on word families. When you record a new word in your notebook, make sure to write down any other forms from its word family.

1 Complete the table below. Sometimes there is more than one possible answer. Use a dictionary to help you.

noun	verb	adjective	adverb
		abandoned	
	abuse		
analysis	analyze	analytical	analytically
			beneficially
communication			
	debate		
			domestically
environment			
		involved	
survivor/survival			
		treatable/treated	

2 Complete the sentences with the correct form of the words in brackets.

1 The _analysis_ of the blood sample showed that he was healthy (analyze).

2 _____ animals may find it very hard to _____ in the wild (domesticate) (survive).

3 Owners sometimes _____ their pets on the street when they can no longer look after them (abandon).

4 There is a cure for this disease, but the _____ takes a long time (treat).

5 Global warming is one of the biggest _____ problems we face (environment).

6 Some scientists have explored how birds _____ with each other by using different sounds (communicate).

7 She has been _____ with animal rights for 25 years (involve).

8 Having a pet can be _____ to your health (benefit).

9 I listened to a _____ about animal rights (debate).

10 Many people who are _____ to their pets don't do it on purpose (abuse).

MODALS FOR OBLIGATION AND SUGGESTIONS

Modals for obligation and suggestions

We can use modals like *have to* to talk about obligations (things that are necessary). We can use modals like *should* to give strong advice or suggestions.

3 Look at the sentences below and the underlined modals. Which sentences express obligation? Which sentences are recommendations?

1 You <u>have to</u> love animals to be a vet.

2 You <u>should not</u> give your pet human food.

3 What courses do you <u>need to</u> complete to get a veterinary degree?

4 If your pet is ill, you <u>ought to</u> take it to a vet.

4 Complete the rules below using modals from the box.

> need to   should   have to   shouldn't
> must   have got to   ought to

- We can use _____ , _____ , _____ and _____ to express obligation. This means things that you believe are important and necessary, or the things that are required by a school or a formal authority.
- We can use _____ , _____ and _____ to make a recommendation.

5 Choose the sentence which best matches each picture.

1 a We have to wear a uniform.
   b We shouldn't wear a uniform.

2 a You mustn't stop here.
   b You don't have to stop here.

3 a You have got to buy a ticket.
   b You don't need to buy a ticket.

4 a He shouldn't wear this to work.
   b He doesn't need to wear this to work.

LISTENING 2

PREPARING TO LISTEN

1 Match the words (1–9) to the definitions (a–i).

1 protect	a	not kind
2 Zoology	b	the study of animals
3 domesticated	c	to keep safe from danger
4 search	d	kind and gentle
5 issue	e	not wild; kept at home
6 suffer	f	the situations in which someone lives or works
7 humane	g	a subject or problem that causes concern and discussion
8 conditions	h	to feel pain or unhappiness
9 cruel	i	look for something

2 Complete the sentences with words from Exercise 1.

1 After graduating in _____ , my sister got a job working with animals in the zoo.

2 This animal organization helps to _____ endangered species.

3 People should treat animals in a _____ way.

4 Some wild animals _____ in captivity.

5 The _____ in this zoo are very good. All of the animals have plenty of space and are treated very well.

6 The biggest _____ for many animal rights organizations is the use of animals in scientific experiments.

7 Cats and dogs are the most common _____ animals.

8 A friend of mine has to _____ for his cat which went missing last week.

3 You are going to listen to a debate about using animals for work. Work with a partner and discuss the questions below.

1 What are some reasons in favour of using animals for work?

2 What are some reasons against using animals for work?

4 🔊**1.4** Listen and check if your ideas are mentioned.

WHILE LISTENING

LISTENING FOR
MAIN IDEAS

5 🔊 **1.4** Listen again. What are the animals used for? Complete the table.

	protection	building	transport	war
dogs	✔			
horses				
elephants				
camels				

UNLOCK
ONLINE

6 🔊 **1.4** Listen again and decide who expresses the opinions below, Amy (A) or Dr Kuryan (K).

LISTENING FOR
OPINION

1 Animals should be replaced by technology.
2 People in the cities are too kind to their pets.
3 Animals should have equal rights to humans.
4 Poor people need to use animals.
5 Animals have special skills that should be used by humans.
6 Without animals, human civilization would not have survived.

POST-LISTENING

CONTRASTING IDEAS

7 Complete the extracts with the contrasting linkers in the box. Sometimes more than one answer is possible.

> but   yet   on the contrary   even though   however

1 Animals, like elephants and horses, were used to build amazing structures, like the pyramids. _____ , their hard work and suffering are hardly ever acknowledged.

2 Horses, camels and elephants were used to transport armies and soldiers during wars. _____ , many of these animals died in these wars.

3 _____ animals work hard for us, they are often abandoned when they get sick or too old to work.

4 In modern cities, we don't see animals suffering. _____ , developed countries spend a lot of money every year on pet food, pet toys and health care.

8 Circle the correct contrasting linkers.

1 *Even though / However* I love animals, I don't think people should keep them in their homes.

2 Some people think the reason I became vegetarian is because I love animals. *Even though / On the contrary*, I am vegetarian for health reasons, and not because I care about animal rights.

3 Many people are against animal testing. *Even though / Yet* without such tests, we would not have developed new medicines.

4 *Even though / Yet* people claim that animal rights aren't protected, there are many organizations all over the world that focus on this issue.

5 Many people eat meat. *Yet / On the contrary*, humans don't need animal protein to stay healthy.

DISCUSSION

9 Read the statements below. Do you agree or disagree with them? Work alone and make notes. Think of reasons for your opinion.

1 In the modern world, there is no longer any need to use animals for work. We have developed technology that can replace them. Their situation is similar to using children to work in factories.

2 People often care more for animals than the poor.

10 Work in small groups. Discuss your opinions.

CRITICAL THINKING

At the end of this unit you are going to do the speaking task below.

Using animals for entertainment should be banned.

1 Work in small groups. Make a list of places and situations where animals are used for entertainment.

APPLY

2 What could be some problems that animals face while working in the places you listed?

3 Look at the statements below. Which are arguments 'for' and which are 'against' using animals for entertainment?

1 Animal trainers force animals to do things that are not natural.
2 Watching circus performances helps people to see animals up close.
3 Zoo animals are kept in very small spaces.
4 Zoos educate people about animals.
5 Watching animals is fun, especially for children.
6 Animals used for entertainment are not in their natural habitat.
7 Keeping animals in zoos helps protect some endangered species.
8 Animals should not be used in TV shows or films.

4 Work with a partner. Think of an example which could support each argument in Exercise 3.

CREATE

Animal trainers force animals to do things that are not natural. For example, lions and elephants are taught to perform in front of an audience.

SPEAKING

PREPARATION FOR SPEAKING

OPENING STATEMENTS

1 🔊 **1.5** Listen to an opening statement in a debate about using animals for entertainment. Answer the questions below.

   1 What is the speaker's opinion about using animals for entertainment?
   2 What arguments are used by the speaker?
   3 What examples are given to support each argument?
   4 What information is given at the end of the presentation?

Using signposting language to help the audience

Good speakers use signposting phrases (*for example, first of all, to summarize*) to organize their arguments. These phrases are like road signs – they help the listeners understand where the presentation is going and help the listeners understand your main points.

---

2 🔊 **1.5** Listen again. Which phrases does the speaker use?

   1 Firstly,
   2 First of all,
   3 Furthermore,
   4 It's crucial to remember that ...
   5 It is well-known that ...
   6 Secondly,
   7 Another point is that ...
   8 To sum up,
   9 In conclusion,
   10 To summarize the main points,
   11 In short,
   12 Finally,

3 Work with a partner and discuss the questions below.

   1 Which phrases from Exercise 2 introduce the first argument?
   2 Which phrases add another idea?
   3 Which phrases summarize the main arguments?

PRONUNCIATION FOR SPEAKING

4 Listen to the extracts below. Notice how the signposting phrases in bold are pronounced as one complete phrase. Underline the stressed syllable in each signposting phrase.

1 **<u>First</u> of all**, keeping animals in zoos helps protect them.
2 **For example**, many animal species such as the giant panda or the snow leopard are endangered.
3 **Another point is that** zoos have an important educational role.
4 **To summarize the main points**, zoos help protect animals and educate us.
5 **Finally**, modern zoos are comfortable, safe places for wild animals.

5 Listen again and practise saying the sentences.

Introducing examples

We can use signposting phrases to introduce examples.

Zoos are educational. **For example,** children can see animals up close.
Zoos play an important role. **For instance,** they look after a lot of endangered species.
Zoos teach us about endangered animals, **such as** the panda or snow leopard.

6 Work with a partner. Add your own examples to the arguments below.

1 I think that zoos are sometimes good for animals. For example, ...
2 You can see many exotic animals in zoos, such as ...
3 Animals are sometimes unhappy in zoos. For instance, ...

Expressing general beliefs

In a debate or discussion, we can use phrases like *It's believed that* ... to talk about what most people think or believe. This is useful, because it shows that the idea is not only your idea.

It is **often said that** animals have feelings.
It's believed that animals can communicate.
It's widely known that animals in zoos are not as happy as in the wild.

7 Work with a partner. Complete the sentences below with your own ideas.

1 It's often said that ...
2 It's believed that ...
3 It's widely known that ...

SPEAKING TASK

You are going to prepare a two-minute opening statement for a debate on the topic below.

> Using animals for entertainment should be banned.

1 Decide whether you are for or against using animals for entertainment. Think of some arguments and make notes.

2 Choose the three strongest arguments from your notes and add examples.

3 Prepare your final notes. Follow the organization below.

- say which side of the debate you support – for or against
- first argument + example
- second argument + example
- third argument + example
- summary
- your recommendation

4 Work with a partner. Take turns to practice your opening statements.

5 Give feedback on your partner's statement. Use the ideas below.

1 Is it clear whether the speaker is for or against the topic?
2 Does the speaker use signposting phrases to help the listener?
3 Does the speaker use examples to support arguments?
4 How can the speaker improve the presentation?

6 Work in small groups. Take turns to present your opening statements.

TASK CHECKLIST	✔
Did you use appropriate intonation in lists?	
Did you use modals for obligation and suggestions?	
Did you use linkers to contrast ideas?	
Did you support arguments with examples?	
Did you use appropriate signposting language?	

OBJECTIVES REVIEW

I can ...

watch and understand a video about a wildlife organization.	very well	not very well
take notes.	very well	not very well
use signposting language.	very well	not very well
introduce examples.	very well	not very well
express general beliefs.	very well	not very well
give an opening statement in a debate.	very well	not very well

WORDLIST

UNIT VOCABULARY		ACADEMIC VOCABULARY	
abuse (n)	protect (v)	abandon (v)	realize (v)
conservation (n)	relocate (v)	analyze (v)	results (n)
cruel (adj)	savannah (n)	benefit (v)	survive (v)
debate (v)	search for (v)	communicate (v)	
emergencies (n)	sedate (v)	conditions (n)	
feed (v)	specialization (n)	convince (v)	
harmless (adj)	suffer (v)	diagnose (v)	
herd (n)	take care (v)	domestic (adj)	
humane (adj)	treat (v)	environment (n)	
issue (n)	wildlife (n)	involve (v)	
poisonous (adj)	Zoology (n)	issue (n)	

LEARNING OBJECTIVES

Watch and listen	Watch and understand a video about traditions in Japan
Listening skills	Identify cause and effect
Speaking skills	Take turns in a discussion; use adverbs for emphasis
Speaking task	Take part in a debate

UNL○CK YOUR KNOWLEDGE

Work in small groups. Think of an interesting tradition from another country. Discuss the questions below.

1 Which country is it from?
2 What is the tradition?
3 Do you have a similar tradition in your country?

WATCH AND LISTEN

PREPARING TO WATCH

UNDERSTANDING
KEY VOCABULARY

1 Look at the sentences below. Then match the words in bold to the definitions (a–h).

1 My grandparents have a very strong sense of cultural **identity**. They taught me about our customs and traditions to make sure that they don't **die out**.

2 For centuries, women in my hometown used to be **pearl** divers, but the new **generation** does not want to keep this tradition **alive**. They prefer to work in the city.

3 The average **life expectancy** in Japan is 83.

4 The children **dived** off the bridge and into the river.

5 The **blossom** appears every year in the spring.

a continue to exist; to live
b all the people of the same age within a society
c a small, round, usually white object that is used to make jewellery
d who you are and what makes you different from others
e jump into the water
f the length of time a person is likely to live
g flowers that appear on trees
h to become less common and finally stop existing

PREDICTING FROM
VISUALS

2 You are going to watch a video about traditions in Japan. Before watching, look at the photographs. Discuss the questions below in small groups.

1 Describe what you can see in the photographs.
2 What traditions can you see?

3 ▶ Watch the video and check your answers.

WHILE WATCHING

4 ▶ Watch again. Which things are mentioned in the video?

1 The population of Japan.
2 The average age of people in Japan.
3 What old Japanese men do.
4 Why only old women dive.
5 When the Cherry Blossom Festival takes place.
6 Who joins in the celebrations.
7 What people can buy in the Cherry Blossom Festival.
8 What happens in the Cherry Blossom Festival.

UNDERSTANDING
MAIN IDEAS

5 Read the sentences below. Write true (T) or false (F) next to the statements below.

1 In Japan, the average life expectancy for women is 79.
2 Women usually live longer than men.
3 The main island of Japan is called Toba.
4 *Ama* means 'diver'.
5 White clothing protects the divers from shark attacks.
6 *Ama* mostly dive for pearls.
7 The Cherry Blossom Festival is in the winter.
8 Only older people celebrate this tradition.

UNDERSTANDING
DETAIL

6 ▶ Watch the video again and check your answers.

DISCUSSION

7 Work with a partner. Discuss the questions below.

1 What activities do old people do in your country?
2 In your country, are there any celebrations which are enjoyed by the whole population?
3 Do you have traditions in your country which celebrate the seasons (e.g. spring or autumn)?

PREPARING TO LISTEN

UNDERSTANDING
KEY VOCABULARY

1 Look at the words in bold and circle the correct answer.

1 A **multicultural** society is a society with *one culture / many different cultures*.
2 When a tradition **dies out**, it *no longer exists / changes into something else*.
3 When people **interact** with each other, they *avoid each other / do things together*.
4 When you **adapt** to something, you *reject / get used to* it.
5 **An invention** is something that is *made for the first time / not used every day*.
6 To **affect** something, means to *make it better / cause it to change*.
7 **Anthropology** is the study of *men / human culture and society*.
8 An **anniversary** is an event when you celebrate *a holiday / an important date in the past*.

PREDICTING
CONTENT

2 🔊 **2.1** Listen to an advert for a radio programme. Answer the questions.

1 Who is Robert Lee?
2 What is the programme about?
3 When can you listen to this programme?

WHILE LISTENING

LISTENING FOR
MAIN IDEAS

UNLOCK
ONLINE

3 🔊 **2.2** Listen to the radio programme. Which tradition in the pictures below is not mentioned by the speaker?

4 Listen again. Choose the best answer for the questions below.

1 What is Professor Lee most interested in?
   a languages
   b cultures
2 Why does he talk about his family?
   a He is proud of his parents.
   b To explain why he decided to study Anthropology.
3 What does he think about customs and traditions?
   a He thinks that they are not important in the modern world.
   b He is certain that they always change.
4 Why does he mention 'technology'?
   a To show how new inventions have changed our customs.
   b To explain that customs don't change.
5 What does he think about using technology to interact with others?
   a It's a waste of time
   b It's normal.
6 Which two things have changed the way we prepare food?
   a books and restaurants
   b kitchen tools and supermarkets

PRONUNCIATION FOR LISTENING

5 🔊 **2.3** Listen to extracts from the programme. Pay attention to the /t/ and /d/ sounds below. Which sounds can you hear clearly?

1 I study different cultures around the world and how social and political changes affect these cultures.
2 My book is about the effect of modern technology on traditions around the world.
3 People spent a lot of time and effort preparing special meals.

6 🔊 **2.4** Listen and practise saying the sentences below. Pay attention to /t/ and /d/ in final position.

1 Growing up in different cultures helps you realize that customs and traditions are often local.
2 We still spend time interacting with other people, but it's not always face-to-face.
3 In the past, people sent each other cards to celebrate important events like birthdays or anniversaries.
4 Traditions don't always die out – but customs and traditions do change and adapt to the modern world.

POST-LISTENING

Identifying cause and effect

During a talk, a speaker can talk about **causes**. To introduce causes, a speaker can use phrases like: *Due to ..., The reason for this is ..., because ...*, etc.

In addition, the speaker can also introduce **effects**, using phrases like *That's why ..., This means ...*, etc.

---

7 ◉ **2.5** Listen and complete the extracts (1–6) from the programme.

1 As a child, I lived in Japan, Thailand and Egypt. _____ I decided to study Anthropology.

2 Some traditions die out _____ our way of life changes.

3 Now, _____ developments in technology, people spend more time playing games on their phones.

4 But now we don't have to work so hard. _____ we have modern kitchens and supermarket food.

5 You can find any recipe you want on the internet. _____ that many people don't need recipe books any more.

8 Work with a partner. Underline the cause and circle the effect in each sentence in Exercise 7.

9 Circle the best phrase.

1 *Because / This means that* people spend more time online, our social lives have changed.

2 Both of my parents work full-time. *That's why / The reason for this is* they don't have much time to cook at home.

3 We have developed new technology. *Due to / This means that* our habits have changed.

4 People don't buy so many CDs anymore, *because / that's why* you can buy music online.

5 *The reason for this is / Because of* social-networking sites, people communicate more over the internet.

DISCUSSION

10 Work in small groups. Discuss the questions below.

1 What are some important traditions from your country?

2 Do you know any traditions from your grandparents' time that have now disappeared?

3 Do you know any traditions or customs that have changed over the last 20 years?

⊙ LANGUAGE DEVELOPMENT

SUFFIXES

1 Look at the words below. The suffixes are in bold. Is each word a noun, a verb or an adjective?

1 tradition**al**   *adjective*
2 modern**ize**
3 accept**able**
4 deep**en**

5 develop**ment**
6 special**ization**
7 techn**ology**
8 celeb**rate**

2 Correct the mistakes in bold using the word forms in brackets.

1 Chinese New Year is a great **celebrate**. (noun)
2 I got 50% in my exam. That's **accept** but not great. (adjective)
3 My **equip** is getting old. I need a new keyboard. (noun)
4 The **politics** situation in this country is very stable. (adjective)
5 Please **short** your presentation – it's too long. (verb)
6 I want to **special** in foreign languages. (verb)

3 Look at the sentences (1–3) and the suffixes in bold. Then complete rules a–c.

1 Things that are accept**able** in one culture are unaccept**able** in another.
2 Growing up in two different cultures is help**ful** in making you realize that customs and traditions are often local.
3 We don't have to spend end**less** hours making our own bread or butter.

a The suffix _____ means 'full of'.
b The suffix _____ means 'without'.
c The suffix _____ means 'can be'.

4 Complete the sentences with the correct form of the words in brackets.

1 A lot of people think that it's bad for teenagers to spend so much time on social-networking sites, but I think it's _____ (harm). It's just fun!
2 You can find a lot of good, _____ (use) information on the internet. But to be honest, a lot of it is not _____ (rely). You need to be _____ (care).
3 It's _____ (enjoy) to celebrate national holidays.
4 Some people might think you're _____ (thought) if you don't remember their birthday.

5 Work with a partner. Which sentences in Exercise 4 do you agree with?

DEPENDENT PREPOSITIONS

Dependent prepositions

Many verbs, nouns and adjectives are followed by a preposition. These are called 'dependent prepositions'. For example, *adapt to* means 'become familiar with a new situation':

It took me a long time to adapt to the new job.

It is important to remember these prepositions when you learn new words. If you are not sure which preposition to use, you can use a dictionary.

6 Complete the sentences below with a preposition from the box.

> in   with   to (x2)   for   about

1 Customs and traditions change and adapt __to__ the modern world.
2 People are spending more time interacting _____ each other on the internet.
3 When did you first become interested _____ Anthropology?
4 Due _____ developments in technology, people communicate less face-to-face.
5 There are people who complain _____ the changes that technology has brought to our lives.
6 Some dishes could take up to a week to prepare, but now we don't have to work so hard. The reason _____ this is that we have modern kitchens and supermarket food.

7 Circle the correct prepositions. Use a dictionary to help you.

1 Do you adapt quickly *for* / *to* new situations?
2 Do you like listening *for* / *to* traditional music?
3 When you search *for* / *about* information online, what websites do you use?
4 Do we always benefit *from* / *about* new technology?
5 What is the effect *of* / *about* new technology *on* / *for* old traditions?

8 Work with a partner. Ask and answer the questions in Exercise 7.

LISTENING 2

PREPARING TO LISTEN

1 Look at the words in bold and match the sentence halves.

   1 **Social-networking sites**, like Facebook and Twitter,
   2 There are lots of **rules** in my office –
   3 You can **upload**
   4 The biggest **event** this year
   5 My **behaviour** when I was a child
   6 I like to **share** my photos and news
   7 He's always **showing off** his new car –
   8 When I was young, I never had any **privacy**

   a photos to the website.
   b was always bad – my parents were always angry with me.
   c help us keep in touch with friends.
   d with my family and friends.
   e for example, you can't use the internet, except for work emails.
   f was my grandfather's 90th birthday party.
   g because I had to share a bedroom with my sister.
   h he wants people to think he's rich.

2 You are going to listen to three students discussing modern ways of behaving. Before you listen, look at the pictures below. What do you think will be discussed?

3 🔊 **2.6** Listen to the first part of the discussion. Check your ideas.

4 Work in small groups. What do you think about the social-networking activities below? Which do you do?

   1 chatting with friends
   2 sending birthday messages to people you don't know well
   3 clicking on *like*
   4 sharing videos or personal photos
   5 commenting on other people's photos
   6 inviting friends to play online games

WHILE LISTENING

5 🔊 **2.7** Listen to the discussion. Which activities in Exercise 4 do the people mention?

6 Listen again. Why do the people say these things?

1 Dora: 'Sorry, but that's really lazy.'
2 Dora: 'It's really annoying.'
3 Yildiz: 'I like to see what other people are doing.'
4 David: 'Is it sharing or is it showing off?'
5 David: 'I think that personal events should be for family or close friends.'
6 Dora: 'It's an easy, cheap way to stay in touch with people.'

POST-LISTENING

7 🔊 **2.8** Listen and complete the opinion phrases in bold.

1 I couldn't _agree_ more.
2 Most photos posted online are not that interesting anyway. **It seems** _____ **to me**.
3 **I totally** _____ . I get tired of it.
4 No, **I completely** _____ . I think that it's nice that people post news about exciting or interesting things that happen to them.
5 **I'm not** _____ . Is it sharing or is it showing off?
6 OK, but **what about** when you get married or have a new baby? **Why not** share it online with other people? _____ , **I don't have a problem with it**.
7 Sorry, **I don't** _____ . **I think that** personal events should be for family and close friends.

8 Complete the table below with phrases from Exercise 7.

signposting an opinion	agreeing	disagreeing
It seems ... to me. What about ...? Why not ...? Personally, I .... I think that ...		

DISCUSSION

9 Work in small groups. Discuss the statements below.

1 People share too much information about themselves online.
2 Young people don't know how to interact in the real world.
3 'Friends' on social-networking sites are not real friends.

CRITICAL THINKING

At the end of this unit you are going to do the speaking task below.

> How has modern technology changed the way we interact with each other? What are the positive and negative aspects of this influence?

1 Look at the ideas map. What is the main focus?

UNDERSTAND

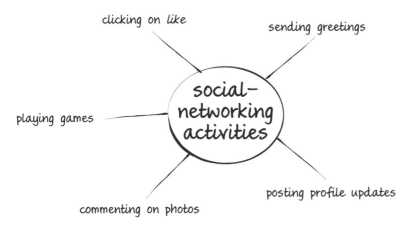

clicking on like
sending greetings
social-networking activities
playing games
commenting on photos
posting profile updates

2 Work with a partner. Add extra examples to the ideas map.

3 Work with another pair. Take turns to explain your extra examples.

4 Work with a partner. Prepare an ideas map on the topic of 'new and traditional ways of communicating'.

APPLY

5 Work in small groups and take turns to explain your ideas maps.

6 Look at the opinions below. Are they talking about advantages (A) or disadvantages (D)?

ANALYZE

Traditions ...
1 are not useful in a modern lifestyle.
2 remind us of our history and culture.
3 give us sense of belonging.
4 help us understand who we are.
5 can be expensive and time-consuming.
6 are old-fashioned.

7 Work in small groups and follow the instructions below.

EVALUATE

1 Take turns to explain the advantages and disadvantages of modern and traditional ways of communicating.
2 Give examples from your own experience.
3 Give your opinions on each other's advantages and disadvantages. Say if you agree or disagree.

SPEAKING

PREPARATION FOR SPEAKING

Taking turns in a discussion

A discussion is an interactive task – speakers take turns when they speak. It is important to stay on the topic and show when you agree and disagree with other people's opinions. Sometimes, you may want to interrupt someone. You should do this in a polite way.

1 Look at this discussion. Circle the best answers.

A: Thanks to social-networking sites, you can keep in touch with hundreds of people all around the world. What do you think?

B: (1) *I'm sorry to interrupt / I see your point*, but how well do you really know these people? It's not like seeing someone in real life.

A: (2) *I agree / You may be right but* in the modern world, people live far apart and it's often difficult to keep in touch. For example, I went to school in another country and now all my school friends live hundreds of kilometres away from me.

B: (3) *Yes I understand but / You misunderstood my point* are these people really important in your life? Of course, you have friends who you meet every day in real life. (4) But *what about / I completely disagree* people who have 500 or 1,000 'friends' on their site? You can't possibly know all of them. And …

A: OK yes, (5) *I see your point / I'm sorry to interrupt*, but I only have about 200 friends. I can keep in touch with them. It doesn't take a lot of time because I can see their updates on my phone all the time.

B: (6) *I disagree / I understand*. I don't think you can really do that. We really only have about 20 or 30 friends, in real life.

2 Match phrases from Exercise 1 to the strategies (a–d) below. Sometimes there is more than one possible answer.

a interrupting *I'm sorry to interrupt.*
b introducing a new point
c disagreeing
d showing you respect another opinion

3 Work with a partner. Follow the instructions below.

Student A	Student B
• You think that it's good to have lots of friends online, and it's good to communicate with different people around the world. The internet is great, because it makes communication much easier. • Tell Student B your opinion.	• Listen to Student A. • Say you understand, but it's not good to spend so much time in front of a computer. The internet is OK, but young people are forgetting how to communicate in real life. • Tell Student A your opinion.

EXPLANATION

Using adverbs for emphasis

We can use adverbs to make a point stronger.

I strongly believe that people spend too much time on the internet.
(= I believe very much)

You can use the adverbs below when you are sure that you agree or disagree.

I totally agree. (= I agree 100%.)

I'm really not convinced. (= I have very big doubts about your point.)

4 Circle the adverbs in the phrases below.

signposting an opinion	agreeing	disagreeing
I (strongly) believe ... I'm absolutely convinced that ... I really think that ...	I totally agree. Yes, that's completely true. That's definitely right. It's absolutely true.	I'm really not convinced. I completely disagree. It's absolutely not true. I'm totally against ...

UNLOCK
ONLINE

PRONUNCIATION FOR SPEAKING

5 🔊 **2.9** Listen to the sentence pairs below. In each pair of sentences, one word in the second sentence is stressed. Which word is it?

1 a I disagree with using social-networking sites.
   b I completely disagree with using social-networking sites.
2 a I think that we can learn a lot from older people.
   b I really think that we can learn a lot from older people.
3 a I believe that children should read from an early age.
   b I strongly believe that children should read from an early age.
4 a I'm convinced that buying expensive cars is a waste of money.
   b I'm absolutely convinced that buying expensive cars is a waste of money.

6 Practise saying the sentences, paying attention to the stressed words.

7 Look at the sentences below. Circle the sentences that you agree with and change the sentences you disagree with. Add adverbs if you feel strongly.

1 It's true that people don't have time to cook any more.
2 I'm against spending a lot of money during holidays or celebrations.
3 I agree that modern technology has changed the way we interact with each other.
4 It's true that travelling to other countries helps us understand other cultures and their traditions.
5 I agree that tourists bring bad habits to our country.
6 I don't believe that learning English affects local customs and traditions.

8 Work with a partner. Compare your ideas. Say if you agree or disagree with your partner.

EXPLANATION

Phrases with *that*

We can use phrases with *that* to introduce an opinion or idea.

I think that ..., Many people believe that ..., etc.

9 Look at the sentences below and the phrases in bold. Then match the phrases with questions a and b.

1 **I think that** people shouldn't upload personal photos for everyone to see.
2 **I've heard that** somewhere in Spain, they have a festival where people throw tomatoes at each other.
3 **I believe that** we should learn about customs and traditions from different places.
4 **Many people say that** travel improves the mind.
5 **I disagree that** the internet has destroyed local customs and traditions.
6 **Everyone knows that** we can learn from older people.
7 **I doubt that** he really has 1,000 friends.
8 **It's a well-known fact that** the internet has made it easier to communicate.

a In which sentence(s) does the speaker introduce a personal opinion?
b In which sentence(s) does the speaker refer to information from other people?

10 Complete the phrases below with your own ideas.

1 I disagree that ...
2 I strongly believe that ...
3 It's a well-known fact that ...
4 Everyone knows that ...
5 I've heard that ...
6 I doubt that ...

11 Work with a partner. Discuss your ideas.

SPEAKING TASK

PREPARE

Look at the speaking task below.

> How has modern technology changed the way we interact with each other? What are the positive and negative aspects of this influence?

1 Work with a partner. Create an ideas map, showing the different ways we interact with each other using modern technology.

2 Decide which aspects of modern technology you think are positive and negative.

PRACTICE

3 Work in small groups. Discuss your opinions.

4 Discuss the questions below in your group. Say if you agree or disagree with each other.

   1 Were the opinions clear?
   2 Did you all take part?
   3 Did you clearly show agreement or disagreement?

DISCUSS

5 Work in different groups and discuss the topic again.

TASK CHECKLIST	✔
Did I use an ideas map effectively?	
Did I use adverbs for emphasis?	
Did I use phrases with *that* appropriately?	
Did I use suffixes and dependent prepositions appropriately?	
Did I interrupt, agree or disagree appropriately?	

OBJECTIVES REVIEW

I can ...

watch and understand
a video about traditions
in Japan.

very well   not very well

identify cause and
effect.

very well   not very well

take turns in a
discussion.

very well   not very well

use adverbs for
emphasis.

very well   not very well

take part in a debate.

very well   not very well

WORDLIST

UNIT VOCABULARY	ACADEMIC VOCABULARY	
alive (adj)	adapt (v)	interact (v)
anthropology (n)	affect (v)	invention (n)
die out (v)	anniversary (n)	multicultural (adj)
privacy (n)	behaviour (n)	rule (n)
show off (v)	event (n)	share (v)
social networking (n)	generation (n)	throughout (adj)
upload (v)	global (adj)	trend (n)
	identity (n)	

LEARNING OBJECTIVES

Watch and listen	Watch and understand a video about people who lived in the Atacama desert hundreds of years ago
Listening skills	Use background knowledge to predict content
Speaking skills	Talk about past events; talk about time
Speaking task	Give a presentation about a historical figure

UNLOCK YOUR KNOWLEDGE

Work with a partner. Discuss the questions below.

1 Where is the place in the photograph and why is it famous?
2 What historical place would you like to visit?
3 Why would you like to go there?
4 What famous historical places can people visit in your country?

WATCH AND LISTEN

PREPARING TO WATCH

UNDERSTANDING KEY VOCABULARY

1 Match the words (1–6) to the definitions (a–f).

√1 archaeologist   **a** a dead body that is wrapped in cloth and preserved
2 mummy   **b** something which is very valuable
3 tomb   **c** someone who studies the things people used in
√4 treasure   the past
5 greedy   **d** the bones of the head
6 skull   **e** a place where a dead person is buried
   f wanting more than you need

PREDICTING CONTENT FROM VISUALS

2 Work in pairs. Look at the photographs and answer these questions.

1 What is the video about, do you think?
2 What is the woman's job in the last photograph?
3 Where is she working?

3 ▶ Watch the video and check if your answers are correct.

WHILE WATCHING

UNDERSTANDING MAIN IDEAS

4 ▶ Complete the summary below with words from the box. Then watch again to check.

> archaeologists tombs buried laboratory
> discover treasures preserved

The Chiribaya are a Peruvian people who lived in the Atacama desert hundreds of years ago. Nowadays, (1)_____ can learn about these people by studying their (2)_____ , which contain many interesting objects. When they died, the Chiribaya were (3)_____ with their (4)_____ , such as jewellery. These objects can help us (5)_____ more about their culture. When the mummy of an old man was taken to a (6)_____ , the scientists noticed that it was well (7)_____ . It was not damaged. This means that he was important to his people.

5 Which topics below are mentioned in the video?

    1 why the Chiribaya people died
    2 how many people lived in the valley
    3 what the Chiribaya people ate
    4 what they kept in their tombs
    5 people who try to steal treasure from the tombs
    6 an old man who was buried in a tomb

6 ▶ Watch again. Are the sentences below true (T) or false (F)?

    1 The dead bodies were preserved because the desert is very dry.
    2 There were 3,000 people living in the valley.
    3 They lived in large buildings which still survive today.
    4 The thieves want to take treasure, such as gold.
    5 No-one knows who the old man was.

UNDERSTANDING
DETAIL

DISCUSSION

7 Work with a partner. What skills below are important, do you think, if you want to be an archaeologist?

	very important	important	not important
patient			
creative			
good at managing your time			
physically fit			
good sense of humour			
sociable			
good at working with other people			
organized			

8 Would you like to work as an archaeologist? Why / Why not?

LISTENING 1

PREPARING TO LISTEN

UNDERSTANDING KEY VOCABULARY

1 Match the words (1–10) with the definitions (a–j).

1	a find	a	to find something for the first time
√2	ancient	b	something (e.g. a body) is put under the ground
3	a weapon	c	something made from wood, stone or metal to look
√4	a statue		like a person or animal
5	discover	d	things used in fighting or war, like a gun or knife
6	a hieroglyph	e	symbols used by Egyptians thousands of years ago
7	a tomb	f	a group of people that fight in a war
8	an army	g	a valuable or interesting thing that you discover
9	buried	h	a monument in which a dead person is placed
10	an object	i	a thing that you can see and touch but is not alive
		j	very old, from a long time ago

USING YOUR KNOWLEDGE

2 Work in small groups. Match the captions (1–5) with the photographs (A–E). What do you know about these historical finds?

1 Petra, the Rose City
2 the Terracotta Army
3 the Forbidden City, Beijing
4 the Rosetta Stone
5 the treasures of Tutankhamun's tomb

WHILE LISTENING

3 🔊 **3.1** Listen to two students. Which historical finds do they discuss?

PRONUNCIATION FOR LISTENING

UNLOCK
ONLINE

Connected speech: weak forms

When we speak fluently, some words are not usually pronounced in a strong or clear way. These are usually auxiliary verbs (*has, was, do*, etc.), modals (*would, can*, etc.), prepositions (*to, for*, etc.) and other small words (*and, you*, etc.).

When small words are not pronounced clearly, we call this a 'weak form'. These words are pronounced with a /ə/ sound.

---

4 🔊 **3.2** Listen to extracts from the discussion. Notice the pronunciation of the highlighted words.

1 Has the professor sent us the list of possible topics to choose from?
2 OK, we can do that.
3 Some of them are human and some are animals.
4 Do you know how old it is?

5 🔊 **3.3** Listen to the sentences below. Practise saying them, paying attention to the highlighted words.

1 It was created for the king of Egypt.
2 Do you know what was inside the tomb?
3 I don't think I can explain the Rosetta Stone clearly to the other students.
4 He was an Egyptian king and he died at a very young age.

6 🔊 **3.1** Listen to the discussion again. Complete the notes below.

	the Rosetta Stone	the Terracotta Army	Tutankhamun's Tomb
Who was the ruler?	King Ptolomy V	Emperor Qin Shi Huang	King Tutankhamun
How many years old is the historical find?			
When was it discovered?			
What did we learn from this?			

POST-LISTENING

7 🔊 **3.4** Listen to two extracts from the discussion. Look at the expressions in bold, which show that the person is paying attention to the other speaker.

1

Ken: Yes, it's here. So, the list includes some of the most important historical finds.

Hakan: **Uhuh**.

Ken: We have to choose one and give a ten-minute presentation about it.

Hakan: **I see**. Let's see what we have here.

2

Hakan: Interesting.

Ken: **I think so**, but it might be too difficult to explain all the weapons they used. **What do you think?**

Hakan: **Yes, you're right**. We need to choose something that won't be too difficult to explain.

Ken: Yes. **I know what you mean**. What about Tutankhamun's Tomb?

Hakan: **That's a good idea**. It's interesting and easy to explain.

Ken: **Yes, exactly**.

8 Match the expressions in bold from Exercise 7 to the functions below.

   1 show agreement with the speaker
   2 encourage the other speaker to continue
   3 show understanding

DISCUSSION

9 Think of a historical place you have visited. Why is it an important place? What can people learn from going there? Make notes about it.

10 Work in groups. Take turns to ask each other about the historical places you have visited.

11 Discuss which historical place is the most interesting or important, and why.

⊙ LANGUAGE DEVELOPMENT

SYNONYMS

EXPLANATION

Synonyms

We often use synonyms when we are speaking. We do this to avoid repeating the same word again and again. Being aware of synonyms can help you understand a long text. It can also help you understand the meaning of new words.

1 Read what Ken said about the Terracotta Army. Look at the highlighted words and find their synonyms.

Ken: It was an army of statues – discovered in the 1940s by a Chinese farmer. These warriors were buried underground next to the tomb of the Chinese Emperor Qin Shi Huang. He believed the soldiers would protect him in the afterlife. I think they found 10,000 of them. Some are human and some are animals.

1 army, _warriors_ , _____
2 discovered, _____

2 Read the extract below. Find a synonym which means the same as each highlighted word/phrase.

Ken: Yes, there's plenty of information about him. He was an Egyptian king and he died at a very early age. Historians think that the tomb was built for somebody else but because the ruler died when he was so young, they had to use it. It says here that it took eight years to find everything that was inside. But from this, we can learn a lot about life in ancient Egypt and their religious beliefs.

1 king, _____
2 early age, _____
3 a lot, _____

RELATIVE CLAUSES

3 Look at the sentences (a–d) and the relative clauses in bold. Then answer the questions.

a This is a book **which explains how the Rosetta Stone was used**.
b The book, **which was written in 2010**, was by Nicholas Lann.
c Nicholas Lann is the professor **who wrote the book**.
d The professor, **who is from Cambridge**, is an expert in ancient history.

1 Which clauses make it clear what thing or person we are talking about?
2 Which clauses give extra information about a subject?

4 ◀))3.5 Listen to the sentences in Exercise 3. Notice that there is a small pause when you see a comma.

5 Complete the sentences with *which, where* or *who*.

   1 Tutankhamun, _____ ruled Egypt 3,500 years ago, died when he was 18.
   2 Tutankhamun's tomb, _____ contained many treasures, was discovered in the 20th century.
   3 The Egyptian Museum, _____ there are many Tutankhamun exhibits, is in Cairo.
   4 The history book _____ I borrowed from the library was very useful.
   5 The farmer _____ discovered the Terracotta Army was very poor.
   6 The city _____ you can see the Terracotta Army is in China.

6 Work with a partner. Take turns to say the sentences in Exercise 5.

LISTENING 2

PREPARING TO LISTEN

UNDERSTANDING
KEY VOCABULARY

1 Match the words in bold with their definitions (a, b or c).

   1 The Ottoman Empire was **founded** in 1299 and lasted until 1922. During this **period**, the Ottoman rulers **conquered** many cities and countries.
      a _conquered_ = to take control of a country after a war or battle
      b _____ = to start something
      c _____ = a length of time
   2 In the **Middle Ages**, Constantinople was famous for its **defences**. A double wall **protected** the city from its enemies.
      a _____ = a system of buildings or weapons that keeps enemies away
      b _____ = a period in history, around the years 1000–1500
      c _____ = to keep something or someone safe
   3 Mehmed II is sometimes called Mehmed the Conqueror because he **took over** the city of Constantinople. He **ruled** the Ottoman **Empire** until 1481.
      a _____ = a large area of economic and political power
      b _____ = to have power over a country
      c _____ = to take control of a place by using force

Sultan Mehmed II

2 Look at the map of the Ottoman Empire. Try to answer the questions below.

1 Which modern countries were part of the Ottoman Empire?
2 What is the modern name for the city of Constantinople?
3 Who do you think Mehmed II was?

3 🔊 **3.6** Listen to the introduction to a lecture and check your answers.

WHILE LISTENING

4 🔊 **3.7** Listen to the next part of the lecture. Write true (T) or false (F) next to the statements below.

1 Mehmed II was born in 1423.
2 After 53 days, Mehmed II entered the city of Constantinople.
3 Mehmed II told his engineers to design new weapons.
4 The sultan could speak Spanish very well.

5 Listen again and complete the notes.

> 1432 – Mehmed II _____
> 1453 – _____
> – _____ to take over the city
> – _____ weapons
> – broke the city walls
> after _____ – moved the capital to Constantinople
> – rebuilt the city – univs. and colleges
> – invited edu. men to live in the city
> 1451–1481 – _____
> 1481 – Mehmed _____
> Constantinople = Istanbul (capital until _____)

POST-LISTENING

LISTENING FOR TEXT ORGANIZATION FEATURES

6 Match the sequence words/phrases in bold with the synonyms (1–5).

> It took Mehmed II just 53 days to conquer Constantinople. **As soon as** he took over the city, Mehmed started re-building the city. **After that**, he encouraged people to move there. **Meanwhile**, he also made it the capital of the Ottoman Empire and founded many universities and colleges.
>
> **Eventually**, Sultan Mehmed II ruled the Ottoman Empire for 30 years until 1481. **During** this period, he became famous for his conquests across Europe and Asia.

1 immediately after: as soon as
2 in: _____
3 next: _____
4 at the same time: _____
5 in the end: _____

DISCUSSION

7 Make notes on the questions below.

1 What periods in history are you interested in?
2 Think of an interesting or important historical person.
3 Think of some important events involving this person.

8 Work in small groups. Take turns to explain your ideas.

UNLOCK LISTENING AND SPEAKING SKILLS 3

CRITICAL THINKING

At the end of this unit you are going to do the speaking task below.

Give a presentation about a famous historical figure or a historical event.

1 Look at the extract below. Underline the facts that the writer gives.

ANALYZE

Mehmed II is sometimes referred to as 'Mehmed the Conqueror'. He is probably one of the greatest military rulers in the history of the world. He was born in 1432, and at the age of 21, he led an army of 200,000 men and 320 ships to take over the city of Constantinople.

2 What opinions about Mehmed II are given in Exercise 1?

   a The writer thinks Mehmed II was not very important.
   b The writer admires the military leader.
   c The writer thinks Mehmed II is someone we need to remember.

3 Work with a partner. Read the sentences below and discuss whether they are facts (F) or opinions (O).

   1 Mehmed II is the most famous ruler in history.
   2 Mehmed II conquered Constantinople in 1453.
   3 Alfred Nobel founded a prize for brilliant scientists.
   4 Alfred Nobel is definitely the most important Swedish inventor.
   5 Christopher Columbus was not Europe's most important explorer.
   6 Christopher Columbus was born in Genoa.

4 Think of a famous historical person. Add some facts to the table.

CREATE

	facts	opinions
Who?		
What?		
Where?		
When?		
Why?		

5 Now add opinions to go with some of the facts.

6 Work with a partner. Take turns to talk about the person.

7 Work with a new partner. Answer the questions below about your discussion in Exercise 6.

EVALUATE

   1 What facts did your partner give?
   2 What were your partner's opinions about the historical person?
   3 Do you agree with the opinions?

SPEAKING

PREPARATION FOR SPEAKING

TALKING ABOUT PAST EVENTS

1 🔊 **3.8** Read and listen to part of a presentation about a famous historical figure. Underline the past verb forms and write them in the table below.

When it comes to explorers, most people think of the great **medieval** travellers like Marco Polo or Christopher Columbus. Or, they may think of more **recent** explorers, like Neil Armstrong who travelled to the moon in the **mid**-20th **century**. However, people often forget about a Moroccan explorer who <u>travelled</u> from North Africa, Egypt, the Arabian Peninsula, through Syria and Afghanistan, to India and China. He crossed the Himalayas and visited remote places like Sri Lanka, the Maldives and the Philippines. He <u>did</u> all this in the **early** 14th century, when there were no cars and certainly no planes. His travels lasted almost three **decades**. And who was this explorer? It was Ibn Battuta.

Ibn Battuta was born in Tangier in 1304. He was a curious and intelligent child. **At the age of** 21, he went to Mecca. In **the 1300s,** the journey from Morocco to Mecca took a very long time. Ibn Battuta returned home after three years because he missed his family. **A short while later**, he set off on his first sea voyage. He left Jeddah and travelled to Yemen, and **then** to Mogadishu, which **at that time** was a wealthy merchant city. Wherever he went, Ibn Battuta described the people, the architecture and the society. He died in the **late** 1300s. However, because he wrote down everything he saw, this helped people in the future learn about past cultures across the world.

regular verbs	irregular verbs
travelled	did

UNL⌀CK LISTENING AND SPEAKING SKILLS 3

UNL**O**CK
ONLINE

PRONUNCIATION FOR SPEAKING

2 Say the regular past verbs from the table in Exercise 1. Do they end in /t/, /d/ or /ɪd/?

3 🔊 **3.9** Listen and check. Repeat the verbs, paying attention to the pronunciation of the -ed ending.

TALKING ABOUT TIME

4 Look at the words/phrases in bold in the text in Exercise 1. Match them to their synonyms below.

1 a period of time lasting 10 years: _decade_
2 a period of time lasting 100 years: _____
3 the Middle Ages: _____
4 next: _____
5 the 13th century: _____
6 when he was: _____
7 during that period: _____
8 after a short time: _____
9 a short time ago: _____
10 near the end: _____
11 in the middle: _____
12 near the beginning: _____

We can say years in the following way.

Ibn Battuta was born in **1304**. (= *thirteen oh four*)

He died in **1377**. (= *thirteen seventy seven*)

Ibn Battuta lived in the **14th century**. (= *the fourteenth century*)

Ibn Battuta lived in **1300s**. (= *the thirteen hundreds*)

Neil Armstrong went to the moon in **the 1960s**. (= *the nineteen sixties*)

5 Say the sentences below.

1 Columbus set off to America in the late 1400s.
2 Marco Polo travelled to Asia in the 13th century.
3 People re-discovered the Terracotta Army in the 1970s.
4 Tutankhamun's tomb was opened in 1922.

Being a confident speaker

Many people don't like public speaking. However, there are many situations when we have to give presentations or speak in front of colleagues. Having confidence is an important part of being a good speaker.

6 Work with a partner. Read the opinions (a–d) below. Then think of some advice for each opinion.

a I hate speaking in front of the class. I get very nervous and forget words easily.

b I think that my accent is very bad. I'm afraid that people will laugh at me when I make a mistake.

c I am worried that I will forget what to say, so I write everything down. But then, my presentation seems boring.

d Other people are much better at speaking than me. That's why I prefer not to speak in front of a large group.

7 Work in small groups. Make a list of five tips for people who are not confident about public speaking. Then share your tips with the class.

SPEAKING TASK

> Give a presentation about a famous historical figure or a historical event.

1 Work alone. Make notes about different historical figures or events you would like to talk about.

> When you think about a topic for your presentation, it's very important to choose a topic that you already know about or are interested to find out about it.

2 Work in small groups. Share your ideas. Ask their advice about which topic would be the most interesting.

3 Make an outline of your presentation using the outline below.

Introduction

_____

_____

Why you chose this person

_____

_____

General facts about the person

_____

_____

His/her achievements

_____

_____

Your opinions of this person

_____

_____

What we learned from this person

_____

_____

Conclusion (prediction, suggestion, advice)

_____

_____

4 Practice your presentation with a partner. Give feedback using the points below.

1 Was the topic interesting?
2 Did the speaker seem confident?
3 Did the speaker use facts as well as opinions?
4 Was the presentation organized clearly?
5 Did the speaker use time expressions well?

5 Work in small groups. Take turns to give your presentations.

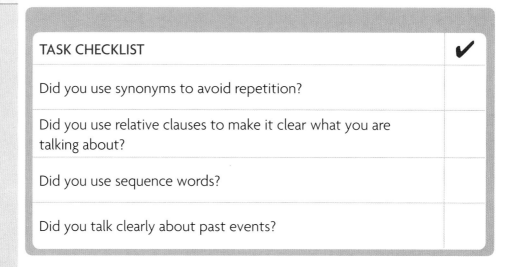

TASK CHECKLIST	✔
Did you use synonyms to avoid repetition?	
Did you use relative clauses to make it clear what you are talking about?	
Did you use sequence words?	
Did you talk clearly about past events?	

OBJECTIVES REVIEW

I can ...

watch and understand a video about people who lived in the Atacama desert.

very well — not very well

use background knowledge to predict content.

very well — not very well

talk about past events.

very well — not very well

talk about time.

very well — not very well

give a presentation about a historical figure.

very well — not very well

WORDLIST

UNIT VOCABULARY		ACADEMIC VOCABULARY
✓ancient (adj)	hieroglyphs (n)	crucial (adj)
buried (adj)	object (n)	largest (adj)
bury (v)	✓period (n)	major (adj)
✓conquer (v)	protect (v)	risky (adj)
defence (n)	rule (v)	route (n)
discover (v)	✓statue (n)	✓significant (adj)
document (n)	to found something (v)	trader (n)
empire (n)	tombs (n)	vital (adj)
✓figure out (v)	✓treasures (n)	
finds (n)	weapon (n)	

LEARNING OBJECTIVES

Watch and listen	Watch and understand a video about the production of BMW cars
Listening skills	Identify rhetorical questions
Speaking skills	Propose ideas; expand on an ideas; talk about personal experiences
Speaking task	Discuss solutions to a problem

UNLOCK YOUR KNOWLEDGE

Work with a partner and discuss the questions below.

1 What are the problems with modern forms of transport?
2 How has transport changed in your country in the last 50 years?
3 What do you think is the future of transport?

PREPARING TO WATCH

USING KEY VOCABULARY

1 Complete the gaps with the phrases in the box.

> robotic arms   engines are fitted inside   reach speeds of up to
> environmentally friendly cars   run on diesel fuel   fuel-efficient cars
> aluminium cases   considered to be old-fashioned

1 Because of global warming, many car manufacturers work hard to develop _____ .
2 Cars that _____ are not considered to be 'green'.
3 In comparison to modern electric or hybrid cars, diesel cars are sometimes _____ .
4 People don't like to spend too much money on petrol. That's why they prefer to buy _____ .
5 The car engines are built from _____ which are very light.
6 In the factory, the new _____ the cars.
7 The cars are put together by _____ .
8 The new car can _____ 270 km/h.

PREDICTING CONTENT

2 Work with a partner. Look at the photographs and the sentences in Exercise 1. Discuss the questions below.

1 What do you think is the topic of this programme?
2 What feature of this car will be discussed?
3 What is the difference between diesel cars and environmentally friendly cars?

3 ▶ Watch the video and check your ideas.

WHILE WATCHING

4 ▶ Watch the video again and answer the questions below.

1 BMW have developed a car which is
   a clean and modern.
   b fast and cheap.
   c old-fashioned.

2 The cars are finished
   a in Austria.
   b in Germany.
   c in the UK.

3 Each car
   a takes a long time to make.
   b is made by hand.
   c is made very quickly.

5 ▶ Watch again and complete the notes below with the missing numbers.

1 aluminium cases – _____ % lighter
2 factory makes _____ engines per year
3 it produces _____ cars an hour
4 can reach the speed of _____ km/hour

DISCUSSION

6 Look at the car features below. Order them from the most important (1) to the least important (6).

- speed
- fuel efficiency
- design
- colour
- safety
- price

7 Work in small groups. Discuss the features which you consider most important in a car.

PRONUNCIATION FOR LISTENING

EXPLANATION

Word stress

Some words have the same form whether they are a noun or a verb.

> Most airlines will not **transport** passengers if weather conditions are not suitable. (*transport* = verb)

> Air **transport** is the safest form of travel. (*transport* = noun)

However, the pronunciation may not be the same. In many two-syllable words, nouns are stressed on the first syllable and verbs on the second syllable.

> <u>trans</u>port (= noun)

> trans<u>port</u> (= verb)

Note that not all words follow this pattern.

> con<u>trol</u> (= noun)

> con<u>trol</u> (= verb)

1 🔊 **4.1** Listen to the two sentences below. Then answer the questions.

  1 They would also discuss the **research** done by air crash investigators.
  2 I decided to **research** it online.

  a In which sentence is *research* a verb?
  b In which sentence is *research* a noun?
  c Where is the stress in each word?

2 🔊 **4.2** Listen and circle the stressed syllable in the words in bold.

  1 **Research** shows that air accidents are less common than car accidents.
  2 We are **researching** traffic safety.
  3 The number of accidents has **decreased**.
  4 There is a **decrease** in the number of passengers flying to Fiji.
  5 The company was **presented** with an award for road safety.
  6 He received a new car as a birthday **present**.
  7 Scientists are working hard to invent safer forms of **transport**.
  8 We need more vehicles to **transport** people to the conference.

3 Practise saying the sentences in Exercise 2.

4 Match the words/phrases (1–10) with the definitions (a–j).

UNDERSTANDING
KEY VOCABULARY

1	afraid/scared	a	to stay away from something
2	turbulence	b	an accident, when a vehicle hits something
3	crash	c	the weather situation
4	cure	d	feeling fear or worry
5	damaged	e	to make someone healthy again
6	weather conditions	f	harmed or broken
7	compare	g	a strong movement of air, which can make a
8	avoid		plane shake
9	safe	h	to think about the difference between two
10	consist of		or more things
		i	to be made of something
		j	not in danger

5 Work in small groups and discuss the questions below.

USING YOUR
KNOWLEDGE

1 When was the last time you flew on a plane?
2 If yes, did you enjoy it?
3 What was the longest plane trip you have ever taken?
4 Which of the following forms of transport do you think is the most dangerous?

a flying
b travelling by car
c travelling by motorbike
d walking

WHILE LISTENING

6 🔊 **4.3** Listen to the first part of a radio programme and circle the best answers below.

1 What is the main idea of the programme?
   a the history of aeroplanes
   b the fear of flying and how to reduce it
   c air-crash investigations

2 What did Mark used to be?
   a He was a flight attendant.
   b He was a psychologist.
   c He was a pilot.

3 What did Mark do to help himself?
   a He searched for advice on the internet.
   b He talked to his friends.
   c He came on the radio show.

4 Can a fear of flying be cured?
   a Yes, but not always.
   b Anyone can get rid of the fear of flying.
   c No, it can't.

7 Work with a partner. Read the list of tips on how to reduce a fear of flying. Discuss which tips you think are most useful.

1 Learn how aeroplanes work.
2 Imagine you are on a bus or train.
3 Take something to help you sleep on the plane.
4 Learn the layout of the plane before take-off.
5 Go to a psychologist.
6 Don't watch films or TV shows about air disasters.

8 🔊 **4.4** Listen and tick the tips in Exercise 7 which are mentioned.

9 Complete the summary below using the words in the box.

> reduce   normal   damaged   avoid   flying
> wings   driving   engine

There are many steps you can take to ⁽¹⁾_____ the fear of flying. Learning how a plane works will help you understand that planes can fly without the ⁽²⁾_____ . This is because the ⁽³⁾_____ push against the air and keep the plane flying. You should not be afraid of turbulence. This is completely ⁽⁴⁾_____ and can only cause an accident if the plane is already ⁽⁵⁾_____ . Other tips on how to prevent a fear of flying are: to learn where things are on the plane, and to ⁽⁶⁾_____ disaster movies. Finally, you should be realistic and remember that ⁽⁷⁾_____ is much safer than ⁽⁸⁾_____ .

10 🔊 **4.4** Listen again to check.

POST-LISTENING

> ### Rhetorical questions
>
> Rhetorical questions are not the same as real questions. They are used to bring the listener's attention to a topic or an idea. The speaker does not expect an answer to the question.
>
> When we ask **regular questions**, we usually stop speaking and wait for the answer. When we ask **rhetorical questions**, we continue speaking.

11 🔊 **4.3** Listen to the first part of the interview again. Which questions below are rhetorical questions? Which are real questions?

1 Have you ever been afraid of flying?
2 Do you feel scared when you sit on a plane?
3 Are you stressed when there's turbulence?
4 Can you tell us more about your experience, Mark?
5 Did it make you afraid of flying?
6 What was I supposed to do?
7 Can it be cured?

DISCUSSION

12 Work in small groups. A *phobia* is an extreme fear of something. Look at the phobias below and discuss the questions.

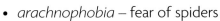

- *arachnophobia* – fear of spiders
- *trypanophobia* – fear of needles
- *ailurophobia* – fear of cats
- *aquaphobia* – fear of water
- *claustrophobia* – fear of being in a closed space
- *nomophobia* – fear of being out of a mobile phone network
- *cynophobia* – fear of dogs
- *acrophobia* – fear of heights

1 Do you know anyone with a phobia?
2 What do you think are the most common causes of a phobia?
3 Do you think it is possible to cure one? How?

LANGUAGE DEVELOPMENT

 UNLOCK ONLINE

TALKING ABOUT ACHIEVEMENT

1 Look at the extracts below. Then match the words in bold to the definitions (a–j).

1 I read stories of people who managed to **control** their fear of flying.
2 They couldn't believe that I had **completed** the flight attendant training and now I was afraid to get on a plane.
3 You need to have the right **attitude**.
4 You can achieve anything if you **concentrate** and stay **positive**.
5 The advice I got was very useful, but it was a **challenge**, and it took me long time to **get over** my fear.
6 The first **method** is to learn more about how planes work.
7 My **goal** was to see the world and I thought it would be a good job for me.
8 Understanding where the emergency exits are may help you **relax**.

a a way of thinking about something *attitude*
b direct your attention to something
c a particular way of doing something
d have power over something
e something that needs a lot of effort to do successfully
f an aim or purpose
g become calm and happy
h get better after something has made you unhappy
i finished something successfully
j full of hope and confidence

2 Work with a partner. Discuss the questions below.

1 What goals do you have for your future?
2 Think of something you successfully achieved or completed in your life. How did you do it?
3 Think of a challenge that you had to face. How did you stay positive?

COMPARING THINGS

3 🔊 **4.5** Listen to the sentences below. Underline the syllable which has the most stress in each phrase in bold.

1 On the course, I learnt **a lot more than** I expected.
2 We can see that **by far the safest form of transport** is air transport and **the most dangerous is** using a motorbike.
3 In contrast, driving a car is **considerably more dangerous**.
4 For me, flying is **much more comfortable than** travelling by train.
5 Flying is **definitely more expensive than** driving.

4 Answer the questions below.

1 Which of the sentences in Exercise 3 use the comparative form?
2 Which sentence uses superlative forms?
3 Underline the words/phrases used to emphasize the comparatives.
4 What is the meaning of these words/phrases?

5 Complete the sentences below with the correct form of the adjectives in brackets.

1 Travelling by train is _____ than driving. (good)
2 In a big city, riding a bicycle is _____ than driving a car. (fast)
3 Driving your own car is the _____ way to travel. (comfortable)
4 If you are in a hurry, it is _____ to cycle than to drive a car. (good)
5 Riding a motorbike is the _____ way to travel across a country. (interesting)
6 Many people buy monthly passes for public transport. It's _____ than paying for every ride. (convenient)
7 Walking is the _____ method of transport. (good)

6 Choose the sentences in Exercise 5 that you agree with. Change the other sentences so that they are true for you. Add phrases for emphasis, if possible.

7 Work with a partner and discuss your sentences. Give reasons for your opinions.

> Travelling by train is definitely better than driving! You can read or work on a train, and you can enjoy the view.

PREPARING TO LISTEN

UNDERSTANDING
KEY VOCABULARY

1 Complete the sentences (1–10) with words from the box.

> convenience   experience   hit   injured   overtake   respect
> lanes   heavy fine   prevent   break the law

1 New drivers often have little _____ of driving on the highway.
2 In the last year, the number of bicycles _____ by cars has increased.
3 Many people drive cars to work because of the _____ of sitting comfortably in your own vehicle.
4 Many accidents happen when drivers _____ other cars without checking their mirrors.
5 My friend was _____ when he fell off his motorbike.
6 Drivers should always _____ pedestrians and stop for them.
7 I got a _____ for driving through a red light. It was over £50.
8 Many cities have special bike _____ , where you can cycle without being near cars.
9 Some teenagers _____ by driving without a licence.
10 We can _____ accidents by driving within the speed limit.

USING YOUR
KNOWLEDGE

2 Work with a partner and discuss the questions.

1 What are some of the reasons that people cycle in a big city?
2 What are the advantages of cycling to work?
3 What are some of the disadvantages?

WHILE LISTENING

LISTENING FOR
MAIN IDEAS

UNLOCK
ONLINE

3 🔊 4.6 Listen to the first part of a group interview and tick the reasons why the speakers use bicycles.

1 it's green
2 it's easy to park
3 it's cheap
4 it's exciting

5 it's fun
6 it's convenient
7 it's comfortable
8 it's great exercise

4 🔊 **4.6** Listen again and answer the questions below

  1 Which two sentences are true?
    a All three people cycle.
    b Eva doesn't cycle often.
    c Anna only cycles if the weather is good.
    d Liam cycles every day.
  2 Which two answers describe Eva's opinion about using buses?
    a You get cold waiting at the bus stop.
    b The bus is often late.
    c The bus is cheap.
    d Thieves take advantage of the crowds on the bus.
  3 What two problems of riding a bicycle in the city does Liam mention?
    a There is no space for the cyclists.
    b You can get your clothes dirty.
    c Cars drive on the bike lanes.
    d Many cyclists are injured.
  4 Which of the following does Anna mention?
    a She uses a bicycle for exercise.
    b She likes cycling with her family.
    c Riding a bike is tiring.
    d Some people use helmet cameras when they ride in the city.

5 🔊 **4.7** Listen to the next part of the interview and complete the notes.

suggestions to improve cycling in the city:
- *make more bike lanes*
- *make the lanes* (1)_____
- (2)_____ *lanes from the road*
- *police should issue* (3)_____ *to drivers if they drive on a bike lane*

POST-LISTENING

LISTENING FOR TEXT ORGANIZATION FEATURES

6 🔊 **4.7** Listen again to second part of the group interview. Circle the expressions below that are used to introduce recommendations.

1 I think it would be safer if ...
2 In my opinion, we should ...
3 I'd like it if ...
4 (They) ought to ...
5 The best thing would be if...
6 I think it would be much better if ...
7 (They) should ...
8 I'd like to see more ...
9 I'd suggest ...

7 Work with a partner. What could be done to improve your city? Take turns to propose some ideas.

DISCUSSION

8 You want to encourage people to use bicycles more where you live. Work alone and make notes on the questions below.

1 What are the positive effects of cycling?
2 What are the disadvantages?
3 What would encourage people to cycle more?

9 Work in small groups and discuss your ideas. Together, decide on three proposals to encourage cycling in your city.

CRITICAL THINKING

You are going to do the speaking task below.

> Take part in a group discussion about using your mobile phone while walking.

1 Which things below are illegal in your country?

1 using a mobile phone while driving
2 driving through a red light
3 using a mobile phone while crossing the road
4 driving without a seatbelt
5 eating or drinking while driving
6 putting a small child in a car without a child seat
7 driving over the speed limit
8 jaywalking
9 listening to music while driving

2 Work with a partner. Discuss which things in Exercise 1 are most dangerous and which are least dangerous.

3 Read the news story below. Are you surprised by the report?

> A recent study reports that eating while driving is the most dangerous form of distracted driving. The research found out that over 70% of drivers eat while behind the wheel and over 80% drink coffee while driving to work. If you eat and drive, you increase your chances of having an accident by 80%. In fact, these numbers are worse than the statistics for sending texts ('texting') and driving.

4 Work alone and make notes on the question below.

> What can be done to stop drivers eating while driving?

5 Work in small groups. Propose some ideas for solving the problem in Exercise 4. Share your ideas with the class.

PREPARATION FOR SPEAKING

Expanding on an idea

When we propose an idea, or make a recommendation, we often state our idea first and then go on to give more details about it. We can do this by giving reasons, or by giving examples from our own experience.

1 🔊 4.8 Listen to a group discussion about the problem of eating while driving. Which opinion do you agree with most?

2 Look at the extracts below. Underline the phrases used to introduce a recommendation or proposal.

  1 <u>I don't think</u> the government should do anything about it.
  2 I think it would be better if they closed drive-through restaurants.
  3 I think it would be much better if drivers weren't allowed to eat or drink while they drive.
  4 The best thing would be to have more cameras on the roads to record what drivers are doing.

3 The speakers in the group discussion expand on their ideas. Match extra details (a–d) to the ideas (1–4) in Exercise 2.

  a <u>From my own experience</u>, I can tell you that it can be very dangerous.
  b <u>Personally</u>, I eat fast food in my car a few times a week and I've never had an accident.
  c <u>The reason for this is</u> the police can check the videos to see who is eating, who is texting, and so on.
  d <u>This is because</u> they only encourage drivers to buy food and eat it while they drive.

4 Look again at the sentences in Exercise 3 and the underlined phrases. Match them to the functions below.

  • talking about a personal experience
  • giving a reason

Talking about personal experiences

We can use the Past simple to talk about a single event in the past which are finished. We can say exactly when this happened.

*Last week, I **bought** some coffee on the way to work.*

We use the Past continuous to talk about the background to past events.

*As I **was driving**, I spilled hot coffee over my legs.*

We can use the Present perfect to talk about general experiences. We don't say exactly when these things happened. We use *never* if something has not happened in our life. We can use *ever* to ask about other people's experiences.

*I've **never had** an accident.*
*Have you **ever eaten** while driving?*

5 Complete the sentences with the correct form of the verb in brackets. Sometimes, there is more than one possible answer. Can you explain why?

1 I _____ never _____ fast food. (eat)
2 I _____ to a drive-through restaurant on Saturday. (go)
3 Today, I _____ three coffees. (have)
4 _____ you _____ by plane? (travel)
5 I _____ a bad experience on my bicycle yesterday. (have)
6 I _____ never _____ anyone eating while driving. (see)
7 While I _____ , my phone _____ . (drive; ring)

6 Work with a partner. Find out about each other's experiences. Ask and answer questions about the topics below.

- flying
- getting a traffic fine
- driving long distances
- cycling in a city

Have you ever been on a plane?

Yes of course, I've travelled many times to Europe and Asia.

EXPLANATION

SPEAKING TASK

You are going to give your opinion on the following topic.

> Take part in a group discussion about using your mobile phone while walking.

PREPARE

1 🔊 4.9 Listen to a news clip about texting while walking. Do you think this is dangerous?

2 Work in groups of four and prepare a group discussion about texting while walking. Choose one of the roles below.

Student A   You are a nurse. You have noticed that accidents caused by texting and walking have increased. Pedestrians should not do this.

Student B   You are a student. You text all the time, even when you cross the road. You have never had an accident. It's OK to text while walking.

Student C   You are a parent who takes your children to school every morning. Every day you see teenagers texting and walking across the road. It should be banned.

Student D   You are a lawyer. You are very busy and you often text and walk. The government should fine people who text and cross the road, but not people who text on the pavement.

PRACTISE

3 Work with another student with the same role (Students A together, Students B together, etc.). Discuss these questions.

1 What do you think about texting and walking?
2 Should walking and texting be completely banned or just fined?
3 What ideas do you propose?

DISCUSS

4 Work in groups that consist of Students A, B, C and D. Discuss your opinions and suggest solutions to the problem.

TASK CHECKLIST	✔
Did you compare different options?	
Did you propose ideas clearly?	
Did you expand on ideas by giving reasons?	
Did you talk about personal experiences clearly?	

OBJECTIVES REVIEW

I can ...

watch and understand
a video about the
production of BMW cars.

very
well

not very
well

identify rhetorical
questions.

very
well

not very
well

propose ideas.

very
well

not very
well

expand on an idea.

very
well

not very
well

talk about personal
experiences.

very
well

not very
well

discuss solutions to a
problem.

very
well

not very
well

WORDLIST

UNIT VOCABULARY		ACADEMIC VOCABULARY	
afraid/scared (adj)	hit (v)	achieve (v)	design (v)
break the law (v)	injure (v)	attitude (n)	experience (n)
convenience (adj)	old-fashioned	avoid (v)	goal (n)
crash (v)	(adj)	challenge (n)	method (n)
cure (v)	respect (v)	compare (v)	network (n)
damaged (adj)	speed (n)	complete (v)	positive (adj)
efficiency (n)	turbulence (n)	concentrate (v)	prevent (v)
engine (n)		consist of (v)	relax (v)
a fine (n)		control (v)	safety (n)

LEARNING OBJECTIVES

Watch and listen	Watch and understand a video about volcanoes
Listening skills	Understand explanations; listen for counter-arguments
Speaking skills	Link ideas; talk about advantages and disadvantages
Speaking task	Argue for or against building a new shopping centre

UNLOCK YOUR KNOWLEDGE

Work with a partner. Discuss the questions below.

1 Name some alternative sources of energy.
2 Are they common in your country?
3 What are the pros and cons of alternative sources of energy?

WATCH AND LISTEN

PREPARING TO WATCH

UNDERSTANDING KEY VOCABULARY

1 Match the words (1–8) with the definitions (a–h).

1	region	**a**	to be everywhere around someone or something
2	surrounded	**b**	to let substance such as gas or water get out
3	explode	**c**	a particular area in a country or the world
4	erupt	**d**	to burst with noise and force
5	ash	**e**	to throw out smoke, fire and melted rocks
6	release	**f**	the grey powder left after you burn something
7	monitor	**g**	a small amount of something which can be examined
8	sample	**h**	to check a situation carefully

2 Complete the sentences using the correct form of words from Exercise 1.

1 Using petrol in your car _____ CO_2 into the atmosphere.
2 The village is _____ by beautiful mountains.
3 The gas bottle _____ under pressure.
4 He burned the paper and threw the _____ away.
5 The volcano _____ without any warning.
6 Siberia is one of the coldest _____ in the world.
7 The doctor took a _____ of my blood to find out what the problem was.
8 When I was in hospital, the nurses _____ me every day to see if I became worse.

PREDICTING CONTENT FROM VISUALS

3 Work with a partner. Look at the photographs and answer the questions.

1 Where in the world do you think this is?
2 What can you see in the photographs?
3 What do you think the man is doing?

4 ▶ Watch the video and check your answers.

5 ▶ Watch again. Complete the summary. You do not need to use every word in the box.

> volcanologist   Russia   ash   volcanic
> California   volcano   samples   poison

1 Kamchatka is one of the most active _____ regions in the world.
2 It is as big as _____ , but only 400,000 people live there.
3 Sasha Ovsyannikov is a _____ , and is checking the Mutnovsky volcano for any signs of activity.
4 He thinks Mutnovsky could explode at any moment, releasing dangerous _____ into the air.
5 Sasha takes _____ of rocks.
6 They fly to another _____ , called Karymsky. They need to check if it is safe to fly over.

WHILE WATCHING

6 ▶ Watch the video again. Write true (T) or false (F) next to the statements below.

1 There are about 300 volcanic sites in Eastern Russia.
2 Sasha has worked as a volcanologist for more than three decades.
3 The Mutnovsky volcano is over 14,000 years old.
4 Sasha thinks that all the volcanoes are the same.
5 Scientists collect rock and gas from the volcano to see whether the volcano is going to erupt soon.
6 Volcanologists inform the airlines about volcanic activity.
7 Plane engines can be damaged by flying through ash clouds.
8 Sasha knew that Karymsky was about to erupt.

DISCUSSION

7 Work in groups. Discuss the questions below.

1 Would you like to work as a volcanologist?
2 What do you think is interesting about Sasha's work?
3 What are some disadvantages of his job?

PRONUNCIATION FOR LISTENING

EXPLANATION

Connected speech: linking sounds

When people speak fluently, there is often an extra linking sound between words. Common linking sounds are /r/ and /w/.

Her ⌣/r/⌣ eyes are brown.

Do ⌣/w/⌣ I have time?

1 🔊 **5.1** Listen to the sentences below. What linking sound can you hear between the words in bold?

1 I want **to explain** some alternative solutions.
2 Many people **are excited** about this technology.
3 Many supermarkets **are interested** in buying these vegetables.
4 If **you add** the nutrients to water, you can grow fruit and vegetables.

PREPARING TO LISTEN

UNDERSTANDING
KEY VOCABULARY

2 Match the sentence halves. Pay attention to the words in bold.

1 Some people think we should **reduce** the amount of energy we use
2 **Fossil fuels** are a **limited** source of energy
3 We produce **steam**
4 We need to **provide** food
5 A **greenhouse** is a hot place with large glass windows
6 You need to **remove** the salt from sea water
7 One **solution** to the problem of **climate change**

a when we **heat** water.
b where we can **grow** plants.
c not **increase** it.
d but solar energy is **unlimited**.
e for more and more people.
f to make it **drinkable**.
g is to use **alternative** sources of energy.

PREDICTING
CONTENT FROM
VISUALS

3 Work in small groups. You are going to listen to a lecture. Before you listen, look at the pictures on page 91 and answer the questions.

1 What do you think will be the topic of the lecture?
2 What do you think is happening in the pictures?
3 What sources of energy are used on this farm?

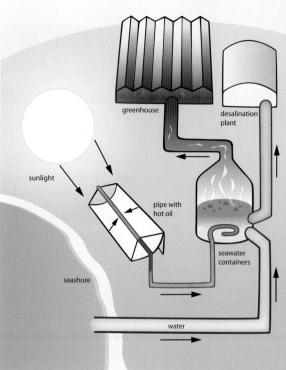

WHILE LISTENING

4 🔊 **5.2** Listen to the lecture and circle the best answers below.

LISTENING FOR
MAIN IDEAS

1 Desert farming uses solar energy and *sea water / traditional farming*.
2 NASA has been researching hydroponics because it allows us to grow food *with more water / in extreme climates*.
3 The greenhouse is heated by using *fresh water / solar power*.
4 Food from desert farms contains *no chemicals / more salt*.
5 Desert farms *use fossil fuels / can help solve the global food problem*.

**UNL⌀CK
ONLINE**

5 🔊 **5.3** Listen again to the second part of the lecture and complete the summary below.

LISTENING FOR
DETAIL

1 The farm is _____ from the sea.
2 Heat is reflected from the _____ onto a pipe which has oil inside.
3 The hot oil heats up the _____ .
4 When the sea water is at a temperature of _____°C, the steam heats the greenhouse.
5 The desalination plant produces _____ litres of fresh water every day.
6 No pesticides are used during the process.
7 This type of farming has a minimal effect on the _____ .

POST-LISTENING

In a lecture, the speaker often explains difficult or new words. We can use special phrases to do this (e.g. *this means*, etc.) or by saying the same word in a more simple way.

6 Match the extracts (1–4) to the ways of explaining (a–d).

1 Scientists have decided to combine the modern technology of solar energy with a farming technology called 'hydroponics'. **'Hydroponics' means growing plants in water.**
2 What we need are nutrients, or chemicals that help plants grow. **Nutrients are like food for the plants.**
3 The rest of the heated water goes to a desalination plant. **Desalination is when we remove the salt from seawater to create clean, drinkable water.**
4 Many supermarkets are interested in buying these vegetables because they are grown without pesticides **or other chemicals.**

The lecturer …
a gives a simple example of what these things are similar to.
b says what group of things this belongs to.
c gives a simple explanation of a process.
d explains what this word means.

DISCUSSION

7 Work in small groups and discuss the questions below.

1 What food do you usually buy?
2 Do you know where your food comes from?
3 Do you think it is important to eat organic food?
4 What do you think are the advantages and disadvantages of eating organic food?
5 Would you mind paying a lot more money for food if you knew it was produced in an environmentally friendly way?

⊙ LANGUAGE DEVELOPMENT

NEGATIVE PREFIXES

1 Add prefixes to the words below and add them to the table.

> caffeinated   approve   understand   government   modest
> known   place   spell   correct   direct   experienced   clockwise
> legal   activate   responsible   mature   believable   frost
> advantage   certain   limited   treat   war

prefix	meaning	examples
un-	not	
in-	not	
im-	not	
ir-	not	
il-	not	
dis-	opposite	
de-	remove / take away	*decaffeinated*
mis-	wrongly	
anti-	against	

2 Complete the sentences below with words from Exercise 1.

1 It's easy to _____ English words, for example *colleague*.
2 He told me a stupid story about how he couldn't bring his homework because his dog ate it. It was completely _____ .
3 The _____ of some alternative energy sources is that they are very expensive.
4 The future is _____ – nobody knows what will happen.
5 In most countries it's _____ to text and drive.
6 It's _____ to drive if you are tired. You can cause a serious accident and go to jail.
7 When I graduated from university, I was completely _____ . In my first job, I really didn't know what I was doing.
8 I _____ the teacher when he told us about the deadline. I thought the assignment was due last night, but it's tomorrow.

MODAL VERBS TO EXPRESS OPINIONS

EXPLANATION

Modals to express opinions

Modal verbs have many different meanings and uses. Some modals can be used to talk about things which are possible (*may, might, could,* etc.). We can use these modals when we want to say how certain we are about something.

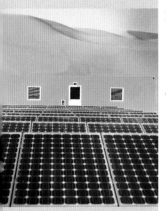

3 Both sentences below give an opinion. How are they different?

    1 Solar energy **is** an excellent solution to global warming.

    2 Solar energy **might be** an excellent solution to global warming.

4 What modals could you use instead of *might* in sentence 2?

5 🔊 **5.4** Listen and complete these extracts from the lecture.

    1 Today I want to explain some alternative solutions that _____ help reduce some of the problems related to climate change.

    2 NASA scientists have been developing this method of growing food, because it _____ allow us to grow food in any climate.

    3 I think that desert farms _____ be a very interesting way to farm in the future.

6 Match the sentences (a–d) with uses **1** or **2**.

    Saying something is ...

    1 possible in the future.

    2 certain to be true.

    a We **could** run out of fresh water in the next few centuries.

    b Fresh water resources **will not** last forever.

    c Solar energy **can't** solve the problem of climate change.

    d Small Pacific islands **may not** be able to survive climate change.

7 The sentences below have no modal. Add a modal verb to express the meaning in the brackets.

                        might solve

    1 Farming in the desert ~~solves~~ the problem of food crisis. (softer opinion)

    2 Not using fossil fuels reduces global warming. (possibility in the future)

    3 Taxing fossil fuels reduces the use of cars. (certainty in the future)

    4 Using solar energy does not lead to any environmental disasters.

      (certainty in the future)

LISTENING 2

PREPARING TO LISTEN

1 Read the information about wind power.

Many people think wind power has many **benefits.** It **provides** an **environmentally friendly** form of energy which does not **pollute** the environment. Also, unlike coal mines or nuclear power plants, they are unlikely to cause accidents and never leads to **disasters.** Therefore, there is a very low **risk** of danger. Most importantly, this **source** of energy is **affordable**. However, **opponents** of wind power argue that the wind turbines can have a negative effect on the environment. They say that a turbine takes up a lot of space. Another point is that the wind turbines are not a **long-term** source of energy, unlike nuclear power plants.

2 Match the definitions below to the words in bold in Exercise 1.

   1 advantages benefits
   2 the possibility of something bad happening
   3 to supply something to someone
   4 continuing for a long time
   5 a terrible accident that causes a lot of damage
   6 good for the environment
   7 where something comes from
   8 not expensive
   9 someone who disagrees with an idea
  10 to make something, like air or water, dirty or harmful

3 You are going to listen to a debate about the advantages and disadvantages of using nuclear energy. Before you listen, work in small groups and list ideas in the table below

advantages	disadvantages

4  Listen to the discussion and compare your ideas.

WHILE LISTENING

5  Listen again and answer the questions below.

1 What are two reasons why one speaker mentions the Fukushima nuclear power plant?
   a To say that nuclear power plants can be dangerous.
   b To show that nuclear energy can help develop a country.
   c To give an example of the long-term effects of a nuclear disaster.
   d To show that nuclear power is usually safe.

2 What three arguments are mentioned in favour of nuclear energy?
   a It's cheap.
   b It doesn't pollute the air.
   c It uses advanced technology.
   d It can supply a lot of electricity for a long time.

3 Nuclear energy can help developing countries in which two ways?
   a They can export the energy.
   b They can buy the energy.
   c They can develop new technology.
   d They can be independent of gas and oil prices.

POST-LISTENING

Listening for counter-arguments

In a debate or a discussion, we often use counter-arguments. Counter-arguments are used to argue against an earlier idea. We can introduce a counter-argument with words/phrases like *despite that* or *however*, etc.

6 Read extracts 1–3 from the discussion. In each extract, what is the speaker arguing *against*?

1 Some people are worried that nuclear power is a big risk. **Despite that**, there are hundreds of nuclear power plants all over the world and there have only been three major nuclear accidents in the last 30 years.

2 Some people say that nuclear energy does not pollute the air, **but that's not completely true**. It takes many years to build a nuclear power plant. During this time, hundreds of machines work day and night and pollute the air in the area.

3 Some people think that solar or wind energy are greener than nuclear energy. **However**, I don't think that's completely accurate. Wind turbines are not exactly friendly for birds. Not to mention that solar panels and wind turbines take up a lot of space.

DISCUSSION

7 Work in small groups. You are members of a town council. You are meeting to discuss a nuclear power plant near your city.

1 Work alone and decide whether you are for or against nuclear power.
2 Make a note of your reasons and think about how to explain them.
3 Take turns to give your opinion in your group.
4 Try to reach a decision that most people in your group can agree on.
5 Present your decision to the whole class and explain your reasons.

CRITICAL THINKING

You are going to do the speaking task below.

> You are a member of a city council that has to decide how to develop a large piece of land.

UNDERSTAND

1 Work with a partner. Look at the diagram. Discuss the questions below.

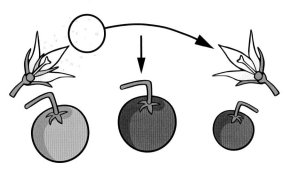

1 What is genetically modified (GM) food?
2 What is the difference between GM food and organic food?
3 Can you find this kind of food in your local supermarket?

APPLY

2 Look at the diagram below. Discuss the questions.

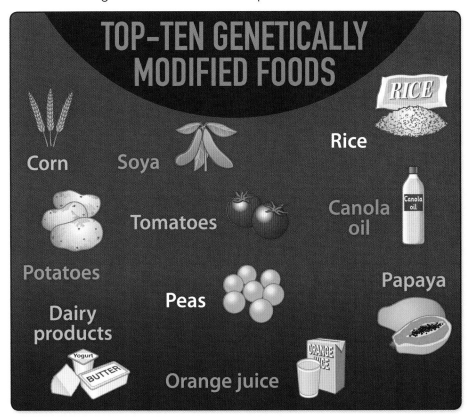

TOP-TEN GENETICALLY MODIFIED FOODS

Corn • Soya • Rice • Tomatoes • Canola oil • Potatoes • Peas • Papaya • Dairy products • Orange juice

1 Which of the food items on the photos have you eaten?
2 Did you know that they might be genetically modified?
3 Do you prefer not to eat GM food? Why/Why not?

3 Read the opinions below. Decide which are mostly positive and which are mostly negative about genetically modified food.

1 In my opinion, genetically modified food benefits people in developing countries, especially where there is an extreme climate, like in Africa. GM food is stronger and the crops are not easily destroyed by heat.

2 I think that GM food is unnatural. We don't know for sure, but it may lead to long-term diseases or allergies.

3 Do we really know how growing GM food affects nature? We don't fully understand yet. For example, it could change the ecosystem of an area and create 'super insects' or destroy other plants. It's an environmental risk. We need to do more research.

4 From my point of view, as a shopper, GM food is not as bad as people think. Farmers have been changing our food's DNA for centuries by selecting the best plants or animals to grow. It helps farmers produce better, cheaper food. And eventually, that's an advantage for the customer.

4 Decide which arguments in Exercise 3 you disagree with. Think of counter-arguments and make notes.

5 Work in small groups. Take turns to give your arguments on genetically modified food.

SPEAKING

PREPARATION FOR SPEAKING

LINKING IDEAS

1 Read extracts from a discussion about building a new nuclear power plant near a city. Complete the gaps with words/phrases from the box.

> begin   first of all   secondly   however   overall
> comparison   the other hand   well as that

A: I would like to say that I completely disagree with building a nuclear power plant so close to the city. To [1] _begin_ with, I understand that modern nuclear power plants are safer than they used to be, and that the plant would be far from our houses. [2]_____ , I worry about my children. If there is a nuclear disaster, our children will be exposed to radiation.

B: I have to agree with this. I worry about the nuclear waste. There are two big questions here. [3]_____ , how can we make sure that it doesn't leak to our water supply or soil? [4]_____ , where are we going to throw away the nuclear waste? I don't think the government should go ahead with this project. Instead, we could build a solar power plant. It would be cleaner. So, [5]_____ , I think that solar energy would be the best option.

C: I don't think it's completely true that solar panels are better than nuclear energy. Solar power is very expensive to set up, then what? In [6]_____ , a nuclear power plant would be cheaper in the long term. And it would create more jobs.

D: I agree that our city needs more employment. As [7]_____ , we need cheap, affordable energy. On the one hand, it's clear that a nuclear power plant will solve both these problems. On [8]_____ , I worry about the plant being so close to our homes. I suggest that we build it as far from the city as possible.

2 Add the linking words/phrases from Exercise 1 to the table below.

explaining a sequence of ideas	comparing and contrasting ideas	adding another idea	summarizing ideas
to begin with			

3 Add the linking words/phrases below to the table in Exercise 2.

> also   what's more   next   all in all   despite that   finally   and
> in contrast   to sum up   although   in addition   but   firstly

4 Circle the best word/phrases below.

1 In my opinion, nuclear energy is safe. *Also / Although*, it's cheap and clean.
2 *Firstly / However*, I think that nuclear power plants look ugly and destroy the landscape. *What's more / Finally*, they don't always provide jobs for local people.
3 Solar energy is an unlimited source of energy. *On the other hand / In addition*, it's safe and environmentally friendly.
4 Wind turbines don't destroy the landscape. *Despite that / What's more*, they can be dangerous for birds.
5 There are many reasons why we should build a solar power plant. *In addition / To sum up*, solar energy is affordable and safe.

TALKING ABOUT ADVANTAGES AND DISADVANTAGES

5 Look at the extracts (1–6) from a debate about genetically modified food. Do the words/phrases in bold talk about advantages or disadvantages?

1 In my opinion, there are many **pros** of GM food.
2 Personally, I think that GM crops **have a negative effect on** our environment.
3 **The good thing about** GM crops is that they can feed a large number of people cheaply.
4 The main **benefit** of GM food is that it allows farmers to grow food without pesticides.
5 There are many **cons** of using genetically modified corn to feed animals.
6 The second **drawback** of GM food is that we don't know its effects on our health.

6 Work alone. Complete the sentences below with your own ideas.

1 The biggest drawback of nuclear energy is that …
2 There are many benefits of electric cars. For example, …
3 There are many pros and cons of using solar energy. For instance …
4 There are many disadvantages of using petrol. For example, …

7 Work with a partner. Compare your ideas. Do you agree?

SPEAKING TASK

> You are a member of a city council. The city has to decide how to develop a large piece of land. Some members of the city council want to build a new shopping centre. Others prefer to build a park.

PREPARE

1 Work in groups of four. Choose one of the roles below.

Student A   You are a parent with three children. You want your children to spend more time outdoors and be active.

Student B   You own a small convenience store and you are worried that a new shopping mall will take away your business.

Student C   You are retired. There are already enough shopping malls in the city. A park would make the city more beautiful.

Student D   You are the owner of a fast-food chain. You want to open another restaurant in the mall and expand your business.

2 Think about the advantages and disadvantages of the two projects from the point of view of your character. Make notes.

PRACTISE

3 Work in groups of three with people who are the same character as you. Practice explaining why you are in favour of the park or the shopping mall. Discuss the advantages or disadvantages of the two projects.

4 Think about your performance. Discuss ways to improve your arguments.

DISCUSS

5 Work in groups of four, each with a different character. Decide whether the city would be better with a new shopping mall or a new park.

6 Present your group's decision to the class and explain your reasons.

TASK CHECKLIST	✔
Did you link ideas effectively?	
Did you explain advantages and disadvantages in a clear way?	
Did you use modals to express opinions?	
Did you use negative prefixes correctly, where appropriate?	

OBJECTIVES REVIEW

I can ...

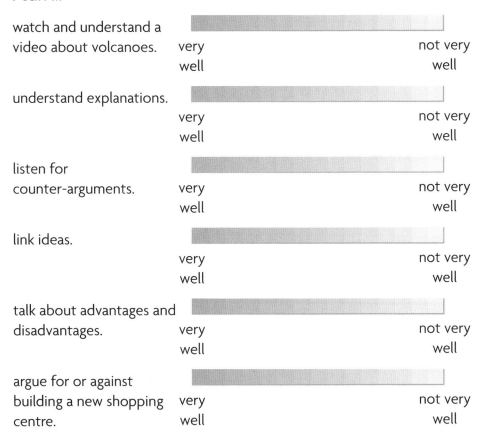

watch and understand a
video about volcanoes.

very well   not very well

understand explanations.

very well   not very well

listen for
counter-arguments.

very well   not very well

link ideas.

very well   not very well

talk about advantages and
disadvantages.

very well   not very well

argue for or against
building a new shopping
centre.

very well   not very well

WORDLIST

UNIT VOCABULARY	ACADEMIC VOCABULARY
climate change (n)	affordable (adj)
environmentally friendly (adj)	benefits (v)
fossil fuels (n)	disadvantage (n)
greenhouse (n)	disaster (n)
heat (n)	drawback (n)
long-term (adj)	opponent (n)
region (n)	pollute (v)
steam (n)	provide (v)
	reduce (v)
	remove (v)
	risk (n)
	solution (n)
	spread (v)
	uncertain (adj)

LEARNING OBJECTIVES

Watch and listen	Watch and understand a video about training for and completing a triathlon
Listening skills	Listen for attitude
Speaking skills	Use problem-solution organization; use imperatives to persuade; use adjectives
Speaking task	Create an advertisement for an alternative treatment

UNL⌀CK YOUR KNOWLEDGE

Work with a partner and discuss the questions below.

1 What do you understand by 'a healthy diet'?

2 Do you do anything to keep fit? If yes, what?

3 What advice would you give to someone who wants to live to be 100 years old?

WATCH AND LISTEN

PREPARING TO WATCH

UNDERSTANDING KEY VOCABULARY

1 Match the words with their definitions.

1	participate	**a**	related to a specific area
2	goal	**b**	the length between two points
3	consist of something	**c**	to take part in an event
4	coach	**d**	to be made of something
5	distance	**e**	a person who gives lessons in sport
6	specialist	**f**	something that you want to do in the future

USING YOUR KNOWLEDGE TO PREDICT CONTENT

2 Look at the photos and answer the questions.

1 What sport event is the video about?
 a a marathon
 b a triathlon
 c the Olympic Games

2 How long is the swim in this event?
 a 800 metres
 b 8,000 metres
 c 18 metres

3 How far do you have to cycle?
 a 13 km
 b 33 km
 c 30 km

4 How far do you have to run?
 a 6.5 km
 b 65 km
 c 16 km

3 ▶ Watch the video and check your predictions.

WHILE WATCHING

4 ▶ Watch again and complete the summary below with words from the box.

> bike   clothes   drowned   light   lose weight
> runs   sea   shoes   swim (2)   triathlon   wetsuit

Rian Ginzales is a computer programmer from California. In order to
(1)_____ he decided to participate in the Malibu (2)_____ .
The most difficult part of the event is the (3)_____ because
he almost (4)_____ as a child. Rian gets professional cycling
(5)_____ and (6)_____ from a specialist shop. His bicycle
is very (7)_____ . It's made of carbon fibre and aluminium.
Rian gets a (8)_____ to swim in the (9)_____ . The first
part of the event is the (10)_____ and after that Rian gets on his
(11)_____ . Finally, he (12)_____ to the finish.

5 ▶ Watch the video again. Write true (T), false (F) or does not say (DNS) next to the sentences.

1 Rian has never run a marathon before.
2 He had a bad experience with a bicycle earlier in his life.
3 Rian feels afraid on the bicycle.
4 His wetsuit will prevent him from getting cold in the sea.
5 He practises swimming 800 metres in the sea.
6 Rian feels worried before the triathlon.
7 He sleeps for a long time before the triathlon.
8 He finds the bike ride very easy.
9 Rian would like to do another triathlon.
10 Rian's friends give him a present at the end of the race.

DISCUSSION

6 Work in small groups. Discuss the questions below.

1 Would you like to do the Malibu triathlon? Why?
2 What sport events are there in your hometown?
3 Do you know anyone who has participated in a sport event? Why did they do it?

PREPARING TO LISTEN

1 Match the words in bold in the sentences (1–7) with the definitions (a–g).

1 Scientists have discovered the **gene** which causes the disease.
2 Your diet **matters** a lot.
3 Research **proves** that smoking will shorten your life.
4 I have a **habit** of eating chocolate in the evenings.
5 He doesn't have a very healthy **lifestyle**.
6 I **doubt** that he can give up smoking.
7 I'm a few kilos **overweight**.

a a feeling of not being certain
b something which is passed from parents to children and controls the child's physical development
c to show that something is true
d someone's way of living
e is important
f being heavier than you want
g something that you do regularly

2 Work in groups and discuss the photographs.

1 What are the differences in the lifestyles shown?
2 How do you think different lifestyles can affect our health?
3 Do you think that our genes can affect our health? How?

WHILE LISTENING

3 🔊 **6.1** Listen to an introduction to a radio programme.

1 Do people who live to be 100 years old always have a healthy lifestyle?
2 What is said to be more important than lifestyle?

Listening for attitude

Often, we have to decide what a speaker is feeling or thinking. This is especially important in discussions, where many people might have different opinions about a topic.

4 Work in pairs. Do you agree with the statement below? Give reasons for your opinions.

Having a healthy lifestyle is not the most important thing if you want to live a long life.

UNLOCK ONLINE

5 🔊 **6.2** Listen to four speakers and read their opinions below. Does each speaker agree or disagree with the statement in Exercise 4?

Speaker A
1 I think the key to a healthy life is to enjoy yourself.
2 There is no question that happy people live longer.

Speaker B
3 This research proves what I've known for a long time.
4 I should keep fit, because it makes me feel better – but I won't allow it to take over my whole life.

Speaker C
5 I'd say that it's always better to have a healthy lifestyle.
6 There is no doubt that bad habits increase the chances of getting a serious illness.

Speaker D
7 No matter how good their genes are, children will not be able to enjoy a long and happy life unless they give up chocolate, sugary drinks, etc.
8 Most of us aren't lucky enough to have great genes, and we have to be careful to take care of ourselves.

PRONUNCIATION FOR LISTENING

Speakers often use a wider pitch range when they want to express an attitude, or when they feel more emotional about something. Sometimes, intonation can be more important than the words we use.

6 🔊 **6.3** Listen to extracts 1–5. How do you think each speaker feels about what they are saying? How do you know?

1 I think it's great news!
2 There is no question that happy people live longer.
3 It's ridiculous to get too worried about healthy eating and exercise.
4 Oh that's great. So now we should all eat fast food and stop exercising?
5 Well, it's great that some people can live to be 100 and do whatever they want, but ...

POST-LISTENING

EXPLANATION

Referring to common knowledge

'Common knowledge' means ideas that most people will probably agree with. We often refer to common knowledge to make our argument stronger and we can use phrases like,

Everyone knows that ..., There is no doubt that ..., There is no question that ..., etc.

However, sometimes speakers use these phrases with ideas that may not be completely true, or may not be shared by everyone.

7 Work with a partner. Look at sentences 1–5. Do you agree with each one?

1 **Most people think that** if they eat healthily, they will live forever.
2 **There is no question that** happy people live longer.
3 **We all know that** our genes are important for how we look ...
4 **There is no doubt that** bad health habits increase the chances of getting a serious illness.
5 **Everyone knows that** exercise makes us happier.

8 Finish the sentences below with your own ideas. Use the topics in the box.

> health   sport   fruit and vegetables   fast food
> smoking   old people   going to the gym

1 Everyone knows that ...
2 We all know that ...
3 Most people think that ...

4 There is no doubt that ...
5 There is no question that ...

9 Work in small groups and discuss your ideas.

UNL🔒CK LISTENING AND SPEAKING SKILLS 3

⊙ LANGUAGE DEVELOPMENT

PHRASAL VERBS

> Phrasal verbs consist of a verb and a particle. It is not always easy to understand what the phrasal verb means if we focus only on the verb or only on the particle. We must look at both parts.
>
> *They spend hours **working out** in the gym.*
> (*work out* = do exercises to make your body stronger)

1 Look at sentences 1–5. Underline the phrasal verb in each sentence.

1 I'd much rather go out with friends than spend time in the gym.
2 My grandfather lived until he was 95, even though he never exercised or ate salads – he was brought up in a different world.
3 I'm not going to take up smoking or eat fast food every day.
4 I should exercise because it makes me feel better – but I won't allow it to take over my whole life.
5 No matter how good their genes are, these children will not be able to enjoy a long and happy life unless they give up chocolate, sugary drinks …

2 Match the definitions (a–e) to the phrasal verbs in Exercise 1.

a to go somewhere for a meal or entertainment – *go out*
b stop a habit, often because it is unhealthy
c start a new habit
d care for a child until he/she is an adult
e get control of

3 🔊 6.4 Listen and complete the phrasal verbs.

1 Who is the person in your family that you get _____ with most?
2 Have you ever had a cold or the flu? How long did it take you to get _____ it?
3 Have you ever signed _____ for exercise classes or for a gym?
4 Have you ever been in a car that has broken _____ ?
5 Have you ever been in a lecture that went _____ for a long time?
6 Can you always make _____ what people are saying in English?

4 Match the definitions (a–f) to the phrasal verbs in Exercise 3.

a stop working correctly
b continue
c be able to like or work with someone
d be able to hear or understand someone
e feel better after being ill
f agree to do an organized activity

5 Work with a partner. Ask and answer the questions in Exercise 3. Ask follow-up questions to find out more information.

TALKING ABOUT PREFERENCES

We can use *I'd rather* and *I'd prefer to* + *than* to talk about preferences, when there is more than one option about what to do.

I'd prefer to exercise and eat well than be unhealthy.
I'd rather go out and have a pizza than spend time in the gym.
Note that we don't use *to* with *I'd rather*. ~~I'd rather to go out~~ ...

6 Read the two conversations below. Then answer questions 1–4.

Joe: Shall we try the new hamburger place?
Mike: **I'd rather** eat something healthy. What about the new sushi restaurant?

Kara: Would you like to go for a walk this afternoon?
Sue: **I'd prefer to** stay at home and study. I have an exam in two days.

1 Does Mike want to eat in the new hamburger place?
2 Where does he want to eat?
3 Will Sue go for a walk in the afternoon?
4 What will she do instead?

7 Work with a partner. Read the information below. Then act out a short conversation.

Student A	Student B
You want to take Student B to a new fast-food restaurant. You really like their food and it's cheap. You don't have enough money to eat in a more expensive place.	You are training for a triathlon and you are being careful with your diet. Student A doesn't know this, and wants to go to a fast-food restaurant for lunch.

A

B

LISTENING 2

PREPARING TO LISTEN

UNDERSTANDING
KEY VOCABULARY

1 Match the words in bold with the definitions (a–g).

1 I like this **scent**. Is it jasmine or rose?
2 Regular exercise can **improve** your health.
3 We have a new range of skin-care **products**.
4 Drinking a lot of water can be a good **treatment** for a bad stomach.
5 Healthy diet and exercise will improve your **well-being** in a short time.
6 If you care about your health, you should use only **natural** products.
7 If you read the label on the cream, you can see what **ingredients** it contains.

a a nice smell
b feeling healthy, happy and comfortable
c not made by people
d the parts of something
e to make something better
f something that is made to be sold
g something which you do or use to try and cure an illness

USING YOUR
KNOWLEDGE

2 Match the alternative treatments (1–4) with the photographs (A–D).

1 aromatherapy
2 acupuncture
3 meditation
4 aloe vera

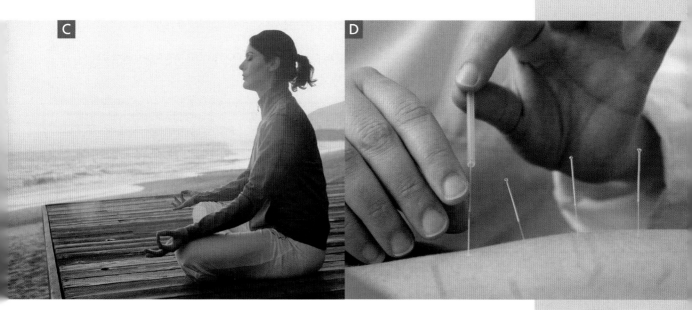

WHILE LISTENING

3 🔊 **6.5** Listen to four advertisements for alternative treatments. What is each one advertising?

> acupuncture   aromatherapy   aloe vera   meditation

Advertisement 1: _____

Advertisement 2: _____

Advertisement 3: _____

Advertisement 4: _____

4 Listen again. What can be helped by the four treatments?

	meditation	aloe vera	aromatherapy	acupuncture
poor concentration	✓			
stress				
sleep problems				
being overweight				
skin problems				
stomach problems				

DISCUSSION

5 Work in small groups and discuss the questions below.

1 Which alternative treatments are popular in your country?

2 Which ones have you tried?

3 Which would you like to try?

4 Is alternative medicine more effective than visiting a doctor?

6 The words in the box are some of the most common words used in advertising. Answer the questions.

> new   make   get   free   best   see   fresh   natural   delicious   full
> love   clean   wonderful   come   feel   special   big   bright

1 Which words are adjectives and which ones are verbs?

2 What products do you think the adjectives could describe?
   'New' could describe a car, or a new washing powder ...

3 Try to imagine advertising slogans using some of the verbs.
   Make your dreams come true!

CRITICAL THINKING

You are going to do the speaking task below.

> The university health club has asked you to create an advertisement for an alternative treatment.

1 Look at two extracts from the advertisements in Listening 2. Answer the questions below.

UNDERSTAND

> Imagine the world of scents. The scent of sandalwood during your yoga classes; the scent of fresh jasmine as you relax at the seaside.

> Aloe vera is the natural choice for your whole family.
> Our aloe vera products will make you look and feel better.

  1 What images and ideas come to your mind when you read each advertisement?

  2 Which advertisement do you prefer? Why?

2 You have been asked to create an advertising campaign for a health product. Choose two of the products from the images below.

3 Make a list of images and ideas that come to your mind when you think about the two products.

4 Work with a partner. Tell each other about your ideas. Which would be most effective in an advertisement?

lavender soap

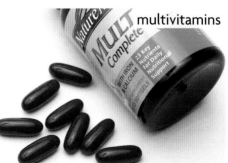
multivitamins

green tea

mineral water

5 Work in small groups. Choose one of the products from Exercise 2.

Make notes about the product, using the questions below.
1   Have you ever used this product?
2   If you haven't used it, would you like to use it? Why?
3   What do you know about this product?
4   What are the health benefits of this product?

6 Discuss a possible advertising campaign for this product. Think about the images that come to your mind. Which of these images would you use?

7 Work with another group. Take turns to explain your ideas.

SPEAKING

PREPARATION FOR SPEAKING

PROBLEM–SOLUTION ORGANIZATION

1 Look at the advertisement for a meditation course on page 117. Work with a partner and discuss questions 1–8 below.

1   Why does the advertisement begin with rhetorical questions?
2   What effect do they have on the listener?
3   What three problems are introduced through the questions?
4   What is the solution to the problems mentioned in the beginning of the advert?
5   What is the purpose of the part of the advert which begins 'As we all know'?
6   Does it tell us what the treatment is good for?
7   What information can we find in the last part of the advert?
8   What verb form is used in the last sentence? Why is it used?

2 What is the organization of the advert? Put the stages below in order.

• specific information about the place, time, etc.   _____
• background information about the treatment   _____
• rhetorical questions to attract the listeners' attention   __1__
• introduction of the treatment   _____

As we all know, meditation can improve your health and concentration. This ancient practice is known to increase your energy and lead to a happier life.

Whether you are looking for a stress-free life, physical well-being or self discovery, Sanjee Meditation has it all.

Sign up now for a free introductory class, starting on January 15.

USING IMPERATIVES TO PERSUADE

3 Look at advertisement extracts 1–6. Underline the imperative verb forms.

1 <u>Sign up</u> now for a free introduction class, starting on January 15.
2 Visit our website for more information about the benefits of our products.
3 Imagine a world of scents.
4 Call us now for an appointment. Let the world of scents take you away!
5 This spring, join our six-month course in acupuncture.
6 Learn more about the course and visit us on our open days on the first Saturday of every month.

4 Work with a partner. Discuss the questions below.

1 What effect do the imperatives have on the listener?
2 Why are they used in the adverts?

5 Change the sentences below, using imperative verb forms.

1 If you want, you can buy our new product.
2 It is possible to buy one, and get one free.
3 You should hurry and book a ticket now.
4 People must not forget that our shops are open during the holidays.
5 We would like you to join our courses before it's too late!

USING ADJECTIVES

6 Look at the extracts below. Underline the adjectives.

1 Aloe vera is the natural choice for your whole family.
2 Our simple, but effective creams and shampoos will improve your skin and hair.
3 Aloe vera juice is a healthy option for people with stomach problems.
4 The warm scent of sandalwood during your yoga classes. The fresh smell of jasmine.
5 It's also a great alternative for people who want to lose weight in an easy way.

7 Work with a partner. Answer the questions below.

1 Do these adjectives have a positive or negative meaning?
2 What images come to your mind when you hear these adjectives?
3 Make a list of other adjectives you often hear in adverts. Share these adjectives with the class.

SPEAKING TASK

Look at the speaking task below.

> The university health club has asked you to create an advertisement for an alternative treatment.

PREPARE

1 Read the information on page 119 about two alternative treatments. Work with a partner and discuss the questions below.

1 Have you ever tried these treatments?
2 What are they usually used for?
3 What is your opinion about them?

2 Work with a partner. Choose one of the products above or choose your own alternative treatment idea.

3 Discuss the kind of images and adjectives that you want to use to advertise this product.

4 Make notes for your advert. Use the ideas below.

1 rhetorical questions to attract the listener's attention
2 introduction of the treatment
3 background information about the treatment
4 specific details about the place, time and/or costs

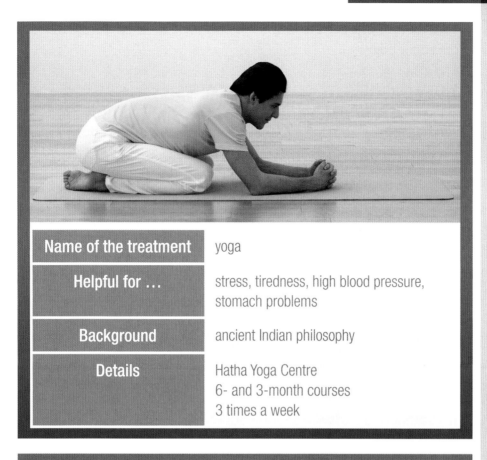

Name of the treatment	yoga
Helpful for ...	stress, tiredness, high blood pressure, stomach problems
Background	ancient Indian philosophy
Details	Hatha Yoga Centre 6- and 3-month courses 3 times a week

Name of the treatment	garlic tablets
Helpful for ...	colds, breathing problems, heart problems, high blood pressure
Background	used for thousands of year by ancient civilizations in Egypt and China
Details	Order from the Ginseng Herbal Centre, Hong Kong discounts for students

5 Take turns to present your advert to another pair. Then discuss the questions below.

1 Was the information clear?
2 Was there enough information about the product?
3 Did the speakers use imperatives?
4 Did they use positive adjectives?
5 Was the presentation attractive and persuasive?

6 Work in small groups and take turns to present your adverts. If possible, make a video recording of your presentation.

TASK CHECKLIST	✔
Did I use appropriate intonation to express attitudes?	
Did I use phrases to refer to common knowledge correctly?	
Did I use problem-solution organization correctly?	
Did I use adjectives to create a good impression?	
Did I use imperatives to persuade the listener?	

OBJECTIVES REVIEW

I can ...

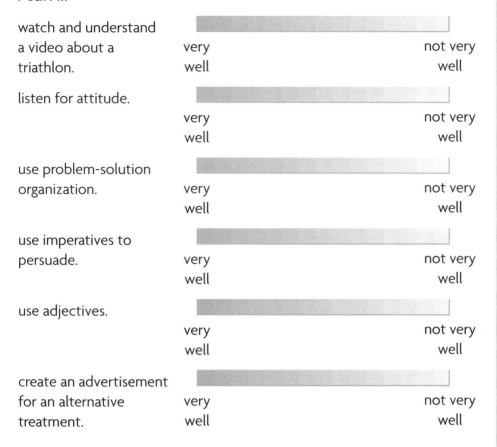

watch and understand a video about a triathlon.

very well — not very well

listen for attitude.

very well — not very well

use problem-solution organization.

very well — not very well

use imperatives to persuade.

very well — not very well

use adjectives.

very well — not very well

create an advertisement for an alternative treatment.

very well — not very well

WORDLIST

UNIT VOCABULARY	ACADEMIC VOCABULARY	
gene (n)	break down (v)	habit (n)
improve (v)	bring up (v)	increase (v)
lifestyle (n)	choice (n)	ingredient (n)
matter (v)	doubt (n)	make out (v)
overweight (adj)	get on with (v)	natural (adj)
product (n)	get over (v)	prove (v)
scent (n)	give up (v)	regularly (adv)
treatment (n)	go on for (v)	sign up for (v)
well-being (n)	go out (v)	take over (v)
	goal (n)	work out (v)

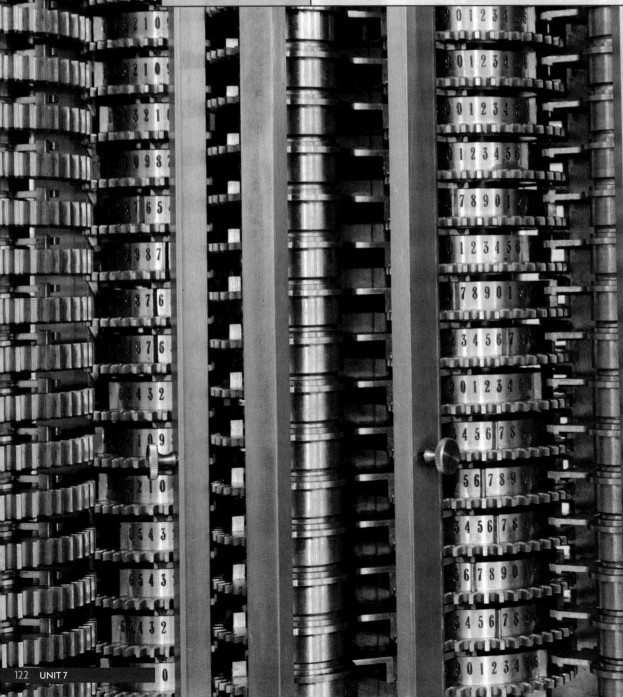

LEARNING OBJECTIVES

Watch and listen	Watch and understand a video about a ski resort in the desert
Listening skills	Understand lecture organization
Speaking skills	Outline a topic; explain how something is used
Speaking task	Give a presentation about an invention or discovery that has changed our lives

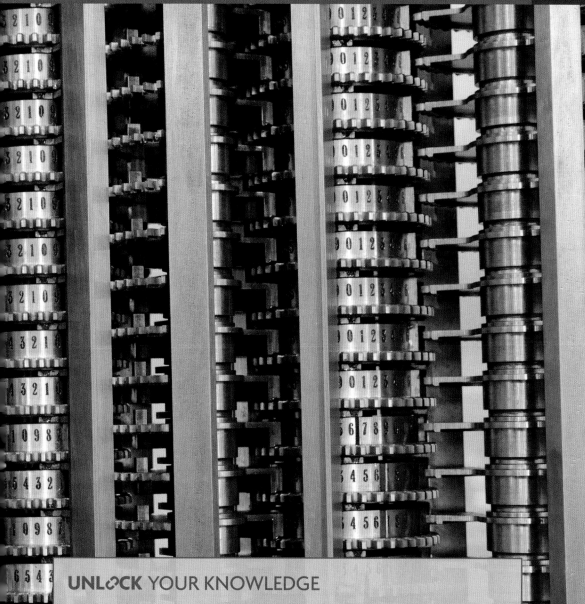

UNLOCK YOUR KNOWLEDGE

Work with a partner and discuss the questions below.

1 The photograph shows a very early computer. When do you think it was invented?

2 There is a saying that 'necessity is the mother of invention'. What do you think this means?

3 What famous inventions or discoveries come from your country?

4 What do you think is the most important invention or discovery in the last 20 years? Why is it important?

WATCH AND LISTEN

PREPARING TO WATCH

UNDERSTANDING KEY VOCABULARY

1 Match the sentence halves. Pay attention to the words in bold.

1 This dry-**slope** is open all year round.
2 The cable chairs **lift** the skiers to the top of the hill.
3 What's the **weight** of this machine?
4 My computer **crashed** while I was in the middle of my assignment.
5 My father can **fix** anything.
6 The water **pipe** in my kitchen broke.
7 This building is a great **achievement** of engineering.
8 We have planned for this **project** for many years.
9 There were no **delays** in finishing this building.
10 The engineers struggled to **position** the metal frame.

a He knew how to repair my bike.
b It just stopped working and I can't start it anymore.
c You can practise there before you go skiing in the real mountains.
d Otherwise, we would have to walk each time we want to ski.
e It's very heavy. You can't pick it up by yourself.
f I had to call a plumber to have it repaired.
g They had to use a computer to help them put it in the right place.
h It took a lot of people and machines to finish it, but it was worth it.
i Everything was done on time.
j Now we are ready to start working on it.

USING VISUALS TO PREDICT CONTENT

2 Work with a partner. Look at the photographs. Answer the questions below.

1 Which city do you think this is?
2 What climate do you think this city has?
3 Is it possible to ski in a hot country? How?

3 ▶ Watch the video and check your predictions.

WHILE WATCHING

4 ▶ Watch the video again. Choose the answer that best completes each sentence.

1 The ski resort is inside the *shopping mall / hotel*.
2 The temperatures in Dubai are on average *under / over* 30°C.
3 Some parts of the ski slope are made *on the ground / in the air*.
4 The slope is stuck in the air because the *computer crashed / engineers celebrated*.
5 The engineers have to replace the *pipes / chair lifts*.
6 The chair lifts are made by a(n) *English / French* company.

5 ▶ Watch the video again. Match the numbers with the information they refer to.

a 600,000 m²   hotels
b 2   rooms
c 900   size of the shopping mall
d 7,000   parking spaces
e 60 m   temperature outside
f 20   up in the air
g 30   jumbo jets

DISCUSSION

6 Work in small groups and discuss the questions below.

1 Have you ever tried skiing?
2 What do you think about skiing inside a shopping mall?
3 What are the advantages and disadvantages of spending money on projects like this?

PREPARING TO LISTEN

UNDERSTANDING KEY VOCABULARY

1 Match the words in bold to the definitions (a–h).

1 Al-Jazari **designed** machines to help with farming. He made drawings and gave detailed descriptions on how to build these machines.
2 Paper is a very **common** invention. People use it in their everyday lives.
3 This museum **contains** a lot of interesting exhibitions.
4 The Chinese **developed** gunpowder and used it for weapons.
5 Sat-Nav is a small **device** in your car which tells you where to go.
6 I have bought a new phone but I need to read the **instructions** on how to connect it to the internet.
7 The teacher drew a **diagram** showing how the machine worked.
8 There is no **ink** left inside this pen. It doesn't write anymore.

a a drawing, showing how something works
b found everywhere and known to many people
c to make plans for something
d a coloured liquid used for writing or drawing
e a piece of equipment, which is used for a specific purpose
f information on how to do something
g to have something inside
h to invent something

USING YOUR KNOWLEDGE

2 Match the photographs (A–D) with the inventions (1–4). What do you think each invention is used for?

1 the fountain pen
2 chess
3 gunpowder
4 the crank shaft

WHILE LISTENING

LISTENING FOR MAIN IDEAS

3 🔊 **7.1** Listen to a talk about the inventions in Exercise 2. In what order are they mentioned?

A

B

C

D

LISTENING FOR
DETAIL

4 🔊 **7.1** Listen again and answer the questions below.

1 When were the things in the photographs invented?
  a in the last century
  b in ancient times
  c in medieval times

2 Why was the fountain pen an improvement on bird's feathers and ink?
  a it was cleaner
  b you could put it in your clothes
  c you could hold it with your fingers

3 Where was the game of chess first played?
  a in Spain
  b in Persia
  c in India

4 Who was al-Jazari?
  a a Persian ruler
  b a Turkish engineer
  c a Chinese inventor

5 What is a crank shaft?
  a a device currently used in car engines
  b a device used for playing chess
  c a device used for washing clothes

6 Why was gunpowder an important invention?
  a people could see fireworks
  b it stopped wars
  c new weapons were invented

PRONUNCIATION FOR LISTENING

Weak forms and strong forms

In spoken English, small words (like articles, auxiliary verbs and prepositions) are not usually stressed. Weak forms are unstressed versions of these words.

The unstressed vowel in these words is pronounced /ə/ (to = /tə/, the = /ðə/, etc.). The consonant that comes after the unstressed vowel is not always spoken, so the words of and or can be pronounced as /ə/.

However, sometimes we may want to emphasize these small words, to make them the main part of our message. Then, we stress these words and pronounce them with a strong form.

5 🔊 7.2 Listen and complete the sentences below. Use one or two words in each gap.

1 Inventions _____ technology from India, Persia, China, North Africa _____ Middle East were brought _____ Europe.
2 _____ game _____ chess was first played in ancient India, _____ modern version _____ game was developed in Persia _____ brought _____ Spain in _____ 10th century.
3 _____ crankshaft is _____ long arm that allows machines _____ move _____ straight line.
4 As we move along, you will find one _____ most important inventions _____ medieval times.

6 🔊 7.3 Listen to the extracts (1–3). Then match them to the reasons (a–c).

1 The Middle Ages **were** an interesting time and they were full of scientific discoveries.
2 Many inventions and machines designed by medieval scholars are still in use today. **And**, some of these inventions are very common.
3 Many people think gunpowder is **the** most important invention in history.

Strong forms are used ...
a to emphasize that there is nothing better or more than this.
b to contrast with an earlier idea that the Middle Ages were **not** an interesting time.
c to emphasize that there is more information.

POST-LISTENING

EXPLANATION

Referring to earlier ideas

We can refer to things we talked about earlier. In the sentence below, the word *it* refers back to the invention of the telephone.

In 1876, Bell invented the telephone. It changed the way we communicate.

Using the word *it* helps us to avoid repeating the same information again.

7 Look at sentences 1–5 below. What do the highlighted words refer back to?

1 The first fountain pen was made in 953 for the caliph of the Maghreb. Before **then**, people used bird feathers and ink to write with.

2 As some of you may know, the Middle Ages have often been called the *Dark Ages*. However, **they** were not 'dark' at all.

3 In this exhibition, you can see models of some of the devices that were designed by al-Jazari. Here, you can see **his** mechanical clocks.

4 The invention of gunpowder has changed the way we fight wars. **It** changed the outcome of many medieval battles and affected the history of the world.

5 Room 14 is dedicated to the invention of gunpowder. **There** you can see early Chinese drawings which illustrate how gunpowder was used.

DISCUSSION

8 Decide which of the Chinese inventions below are most important. Make notes on the questions below.

1 How have these inventions changed the history of the world?
2 Are they still used? How?
3 Have these inventions led to other discoveries?

9 Work in groups. Take turns to explain why the inventions you chose are the most important.

A the compass

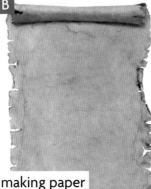
B making paper

C printing

⊙ LANGUAGE DEVELOPMENT

PHRASES WITH *MAKE*

1 Look at the phrases with *make* in the ideas map. Then complete the sentences (1–8).

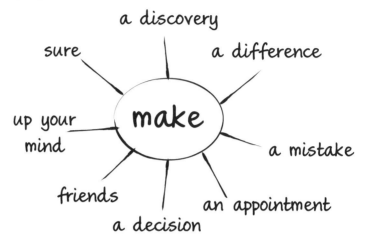

a discovery

sure

a difference

up your mind

make

a mistake

friends

a decision

an appointment

1 Some <u>discoveries</u> are **made** by chance. For example, Fleming found penicillin after a failed experiment.

2 The invention of the light bulb has **made** a huge _____ to our lifestyles.

3 I've **made** a big _____ . My physics exam isn't tomorrow – it's today!

4 Before you start the experiment, please **make** _____ that you follow all the safety instructions.

5 I can't **make** _____ if the most important invention is gunpowder or paper.

6 I **made** _____ with Paul when I met him at university.

7 It's difficult to **make** a good _____ when you are tired.

8 If you want to see the doctor, please **make** _____ .

2 Look at the sentences below. Decide if *make* means 'cause', 'force' or 'produce'.

1 Gunpowder was first **made** in China. produce

2 My professor **made** me re-write my assignment, because there were too many mistakes.

3 Email **makes** it easy for people to stay in touch.

4 Modern eBooks are not **made** from paper.

5 The new discovery **made** a lot of people very happy.

6 I **made** myself stay up late and finish the work.

PASSIVE VERB FORMS

EXPLANATION

Passive forms

We use passive verb forms when we focus on what happened to something, not on who did something.

Alan Turing invented the digital computer. (= focusing on the inventor)
The digital computer was invented in 1936. (= focusing on the invention)

To form the passive, we use *be* + past participle. We can use *by* when we want to mention who did something.

The light bulb was developed **by** Edison.

3 Work with a partner. Look at the list of inventors and inventions below. Take turns to make passive sentences.

1 Apple's first tablet computer – develop – the 1990s
Apple's first tablet computer was developed in the 1990s.
2 the law of gravity – discover – Isaac Newton – the 17th century
3 the first computer chip – invent – the 1950s
4 the first smartphone – create – after 1997
5 penicillin – first produce – 1928 – Alexander Fleming

4 Complete the sentences below using the correct form of the verbs in brackets. Use active or passive forms.

1 Paper _____ (discover) in ancient China.
2 The telephone _____ (invent) in 1876.
3 Imhotep, an Egyptian architect, _____ (design) the Pyramid of Djoser.
4 The game of chess _____ (bring) to Europe from Persia.
5 This letter _____ (write) with ink.
6 A very early calculator _____ (create) by Blaise Pascal.
7 Millions of people _____ (download) smartphone apps every day.
8 The pictures _____ (send) by email.
9 The first photograph _____ (take) in 1826.
10 Edison _____ (develop) his first light bulb in 1879.

LISTENING 2

PREPARING TO LISTEN

1 Look at the sentences (1–8) from a lecture about mobile phones. What is an 'app'?

1 The first apps were designed to increase **efficiency** at work and help people **access** important information.
2 Users simply download the app from the internet and **install** it on their smartphone.
3 Since their first introduction, the app market has grown **beyond** all our expectations.
4 They are, in fact, a worldwide **phenomenon**, as people from all over the world use apps for entertainment, travel or communication.
5 They can **recommend** a new movie, a restaurant in your neighbourhood or tell the weather.
6 Texting has become one of the **leading** forms of communication.
7 There are hundreds of thousands of apps **available** for us to download.
8 Many apps have **allowed** us to stay in touch with each other at any time.

2 Complete the sentences below with the correct form of the words in bold from Exercise 1.

1 Email is a quick and _efficient_ way to contact people.
2 This app _____ you to check your bank account any time.
3 The US and Korea were the _____ countries in developing the first smartphones.
4 Once you download the app, you have to _____ it on your smartphone.
5 The apps have changed our lives _____ our imagination.
6 It's _____ to have anti-virus software on your computer.
7 I need a password to _____ the wi-fi connection in this café.
8 Smartphones and tablet computers have quickly become an international _____ .
9 There are many social media apps _____ for your smartphone.

3 Work in small groups and discuss the questions below.

USING YOUR
KNOWLEDGE TO
PREDICT CONTENT

  1 Do you have any apps on your phone?
  2 What kinds of thing can apps do?
  3 How many apps do you think are downloaded every year?
  4 What kind of apps are the most popular? Why?

4 🔊 **7.4** Listen to an introduction to a lecture. Put the topics below in the order that they will be discussed.

  a The influence of apps on our lives.
  b Specific examples of popular apps.
  c The history of apps.

WHILE LISTENING

5 Work with a partner. Look at the mobile phone apps below. Discuss the ones you use. Do you think these apps are useful?

LISTENING FOR
MAIN IDEAS

  1 translating languages
  2 having access to your email at any time
  3 checking social-networking sites
  4 internet banking
  5 maps
  6 checking the news
  7 listening to music
  8 recommending hotels or restaurants
  9 checking the weather
  10 telling you what's on TV
  11 games
  12 searching for jobs

6 🔊 **7.5** Listen to the lecture and circle the ideas in Exercise 5 that are mentioned.

7 Listen again and complete the notes below.

> *first apps used for:*
> *accessing the* _____
>   *—* _____
>   *—* _____
>
> *second gen. apps*
>   *—* _____ *opened in 2008*
>   *— 2011 – 10 billion downloads*
>   *— 2012 –* _____ *downloads*
> *new apps*
>   *— more people use apps than* _____
>   *— there is a need for skilled* _____

POST-LISTENING

8 Look at the extracts (1–6) from the lecture. Underline the expressions that the lecturer uses to say what will happen next.

1 <u>We will start by</u> discussing the beginnings of the first apps.
2 We will then discuss how apps have changed our lives.
3 I'd like to start by talking a little bit about the first apps.
4 I'm going to briefly talk about how these apps changed our lives.
5 Now, I'd like to mention another important area – gaming.
6 In the next part of the lecture, I will discuss some of the most common apps in more detail.

DISCUSSION

9 Work alone and make notes. Think of an app that you would like to recommend to other people in your class.

1 What app is it?
2 What do you use it for?
3 Where can you get it?

4 Why would you like to recommend it?

10 Work in small groups. Take turns to tell each other about your apps. Which one seems the most useful?

CRITICAL THINKING

You are going to do the speaking task below.

> Give a short presentation about an invention or discovery that has changed our lives.

1 Work with a partner and discuss the questions below.

1 Can you imagine a world without the internet? What would it be like?
2 What problems would you have without it?
3 How did people communicate before the internet?
4 How did students do research before the internet?
5 How has the internet changed since its invention?
6 Has it led to other inventions?

2 Work alone. Choose two of the inventions from the photographs. Then make notes on the questions below.

1 When was the last time you used these things?
2 Are they useful?
3 Could you live without them?
4 How have they affected our lives?
5 What problems did people have before these things were invented?

the microwave

the safety seatbelt

the plastic bottle

the bicycle

3 Work in small groups. Tell each other about the inventions you chose.

> When you do research on a topic, try to ask yourself the following questions.
> *Who? What? When? Where? Why?* Many researchers add *How?* to this list.

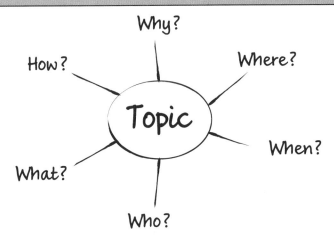

4 Work with a partner. Choose an invention from Exercise 2. Write questions on the ideas map about the invention you chose.

ANALYZE

Who invented it?　　　Who uses it?

5 Work with another pair. Show each other your questions. How many can you answer?

SPEAKING

PREPARATION FOR SPEAKING

OUTLINING A TOPIC

1 ◀)) **7.6** Listen to an introduction to a presentation, which outlines what the speaker is talking about. Answer questions 1–5 below.

Does the speaker ...
1 mention the invention's name in the first sentence?
2 give a description of the invention?
3 say how you can use it?
4 explain what will happen next in the presentation?
5 give specific details on how this invention is used?

2 Work with a partner. Practise giving an introduction about a simple invention. Use the outline below to organize your ideas.

Student A: give an introduction to a presentation about the **paper notebook**.
Student B: give an introduction to a presentation about the **ballpoint pen**.

> I would like to present an invention that has changed the way we _____ . It's a simple invention and we have all used it in the past.
>
> It's the _____ .
>
> A _____ is _____ (*explain the invention here*).
>
> You can _____ (*explain how it is used in general*).
>
> First, I am going to talk about _____ . Then, I will explain how it has improved our lives.

UNL⌾CK LISTENING AND SPEAKING SKILLS 3

ORGANIZING IDEAS

3 Look at the next part of the presentation below. Put questions a–g in the order they are answered in the presentation.

a Why do people use them?   _____
b Who made them?   _____
c Where can people use them?   _____
d Why were they invented?   _____
e When were they invented?   __1__
f Why is it a good invention?   _____
g When were they first sold?   _____

> To start with, post-its were invented in 1974 by Art Fry. Fry needed a bookmark that would stay inside the book and didn't fall out. He used a special type of glue invented by his colleague Spencer Silver. The glue was not very strong and made it easy to remove the notes.
>
> In 1977, the first post-it notes were sold in shops. Since then, they have become a global phenomenon. People all over the word recognize the small, yellow sticky notes. We use them at work, at school and at home. Because the glue does not leave any stains, people can stick post-its anywhere. They allow us to remember important information and take notes. The best thing is that you can stick a post-it anywhere to help you remember something.

EXPLAINING HOW SOMETHING IS USED

4 Complete the sentences below with phrases from the box.

> helps people to   makes it   is useful for
> without   allows us

1 GPS _____ to find our way around unknown places.
2 The mobile phone _____ stay in touch.
3 Email _____ sending files quickly and cheaply.
4 Television _____ easy to learn about the world.
5 _____ the computer chip, we wouldn't be able to use laptops.

5 Write two sentences about the laptop computer and two sentences about the smartphone. Use phrases from Exercise 4.

6 Work with a partner. Take turns to say your sentences. Do you agree?

SPEAKING TASK

> Give a short presentation about an invention or discovery that has changed our lives.

PREPARE

1 Work alone. Make a list of inventions or discoveries that have changed our lives.

2 Choose one of the inventions and prepare an ideas map about it. Write questions on the diagram.

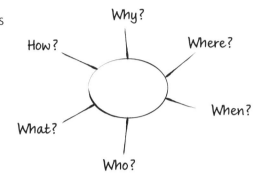

3 Work with a partner. Discuss your research questions and help each other answer the questions on the ideas maps.

PRACTISE

4 Work with a partner. Take turns to practise giving your presentation.

5 Give each other feedback using the questions below.
   1 Was the presentation clearly organized and interesting?
   2 Was there a clear description of the invention/discovery?
   3 Were there examples of how the invention/discovery has changed our lives?

PRESENT

6 Work in small groups. Take turns to give your presentations. Discuss which one of your inventions has had the biggest influence on our lives.

TASK CHECKLIST	✔
Did you use phrases with *make* correctly?	
Did you use passive and active forms correctly?	
Did you outline the topic clearly?	
Did you explain clearly how something is used?	

OBJECTIVES REVIEW

I can ...

watch and understand a video about a ski resort in the desert.

very well — not very well

understand lecture organization.

very well — not very well

outline a topic.

very well — not very well

explain how something is used.

very well — not very well

give a presentation about an invention or discovery that has changed our lives.

very well — not very well

WORDLIST

UNIT VOCABULARY		ACADEMIC VOCABULARY
achievement (n)	install (v)	contain (v)
allow (v)	instruction (n)	design (v)
available (adj)	launch (v)	develop (v)
beyond (adv)	lift (v)	diagram (n)
common (adj)	phenomenon (n)	make a difference (v)
delay (n)	position (n)	make a discovery (v)
device (n)	recommend (v)	make a mistake (v)
efficiency (n)	weapon (n)	make sure (v)
fix (v)	weight (n)	
ink (n)		

LEARNING OBJECTIVES

Watch and listen	Watch and understand a video about how clothes become fashionable
Listening skills	Use visuals to predict information
Speaking skills	Ask for opinions; check information; focus on information coming next
Speaking task	Interview people to find out attitudes towards dress codes

UNL**O**CK YOUR KNOWLEDGE

Work with a partner and discuss the questions below.

1 Is fashion important in your life?
2 What do young people like to wear in your country at the moment?
3 Has fashion changed a lot in your country in the last 50 years?

WATCH AND LISTEN

PREPARE TO WATCH

UNDERSTANDING
KEY VOCABULARY

1 Complete the sentences with the words in the box.

> fashionable   practical   patterns   tracksuits
> workshop   woollen   stains   denim

1 Stella McCartney designed the _____ for the British Olympic team in 2012.
2 Levi Strauss invented the first jeans which were made from _____ .
3 Some clothes become more _____ when celebrities and famous sports stars wear them.
4 I usually wear clothes with bold, bright clothes, with colourful _____ .
5 I often wear _____ clothes in the winter, like hats, scarves, pullovers.
6 Heavy boots are not very _____ for running.
7 Most fashion designers have a _____ where they make their clothes.
8 It's better not to wear white clothes, because if you get them dirty, you can see the _____ .

PREDICTING
CONTENT

2 Work with a partner and discuss the questions below.

1 Make a list of five pieces of practical clothing (e.g. gloves, hard-wearing trousers, etc.). Can these clothes also be fashionable?
2 When do people wear tracksuits? Do only sportspeople wear them?
3 Why are running shoes fashionable, do you think?
4 Why were jeans invented, do you think? Who first wore them?

3 ▶ Watch the video and compare your ideas.

WHILE WATCHING

4 ▶ Complete the summary with words in the box.

> fit   stylish   jogging   material   Olympics   celebrities

Many of the clothes which are (1)_____ today actually started as practical items. For example, Ottavio Missoni invented the tracksuit for the 1948 (2)_____ . After that, he made more tracksuits from wool, and they became popular because of their comfortable (3)_____ .

Other sports clothes, like running shoes, also became popular. In the 1970s, (4)_____ became a popular sport and people needed these shoes. By the 1980s, these shoes became popular with (5)_____ , and people started wearing them for everyday use – not just for running.

Another example of everyday clothes which became fashionable are jeans. Levi Strauss invented these for Californian miners to wear. The miners needed hard-wearing clothes which were made of a strong (6)_____ . He made his jeans a dark blue to hide the stains. Jeans were worn by manual workers until the 1950s and 60s, when movie stars started to wear them.

5 ▶ Watch again. Write true (T) or false (F) or does not say (DNS) next to the statements below.

1 Missoni was a sportsman as well as a designer.
2 Missoni only make tracksuits.
3 Popular fashion designers like Stella McCartney have created tracksuits.
4 More people were running in the 1980s than the 1970s.
5 Celebrities were used to advertise running shoes.
6 Levi Strauss started his career by making clothes.
7 His original jeans for miners were made of denim.
8 Marlon Brando and James Dean started their careers as manual workers.

DISCUSSION

6 Work in small groups. Discuss the questions below.

1 Which is more important when you buy clothes: that they are practical, or that they are stylish?
2 What clothes are fashionable in your country right now?
3 Are jeans, running shoes and tracksuits popular?
4 Why are jeans so popular around the world?
5 In your culture, is it OK to wear jeans or running shoes in formal situations, like at work? Why/Why not?

PREPARING TO LISTEN

1 Match the words/phrases (1–9) with the definitions (a–i).

1 Our clothes are made from 100% natural **fabric**.
2 My **local** shopping centre has lots of great clothes shops.
3 The prisoners were kept in very poor **conditions**.
4 Solar panels **convert** sunlight into energy.
5 My wife **collects** shoes – she has more than 20 pairs.
6 **There is no point** buying designer clothes – just buy cheap ones.
7 These shoes are not **practical** – I can't walk in them!
8 The **focus** of this exhibition is fashion and design.
9 I like the **design** of this dress.

a change something into something else
b cloth, material
c related to an area near you
d the situation in which people work and live
e suitable for the situation in which something is used
f the part which gets the most attention
g get things from different places and bring them together
h there is no good reason or purpose for something
i a pattern or decoration

2 You are going to listen to a discussion about clothes. Before you listen, look at the photograph. What do you think the discussion will focus on?

3 Work in small groups. Look at the predictions below about clothes in the future. Discuss which predictions you think might come true.

In the future …
1 our clothes will fight air pollution.
2 our clothes will be made from recycled materials.
3 clothes will clean themselves.
4 we will be able to charge phone batteries from our clothes.
5 there will be clothes that make you almost invisible.
6 our clothes will be able to reduce pain.
7 clothes will be made of metal.
8 our clothes will be able to kill bacteria.
9 our clothes will use electricity.
10 our clothes will speak to us.

WHILE LISTENING

4 🔊 **8.1** Listen to two students discussing the future of clothes. Circle the ideas in Exercise 3 that they mention.

LISTENING FOR
MAIN IDEAS

PRONUNCIATION FOR LISTENING

Vowel elision

Sometimes, we do not pronounce every letter in a word. Unstressed vowels are not always pronounced when they appear between a consonant and /l/ or /r/.

5 🔊 **8.2** Listen to the extracts below. Focus on the words in bold. Circle the vowels that are not pronounced.

1 I've been looking for an int**e**resting topic, but to be honest, I've found nothing in the **library**.
2 So in the future, we could use this fabric to charge our mobile phones, our **cameras** or other small devices as we walk, is that right?
3 Well, these fabrics keep your body **temperature** the same whatever the weather. They can be used to make sports clothing.
4 So, we have clothes that are **environmentally** friendly.
5 There are a lot of **different** articles on this topic.

6 Listen again. Practise saying the sentences in Exercise 5.

7 🔊 **8.1** Listen to the discussion again and answer the questions below.

1 Eco-friendly designers ...
   a help poor communities.
   b recycle their clothes.
   c protect endangered animals.
2 Some scientists are working on clothes that ...
   a can use bacteria.
   b use electricity.
   c can make phone calls.
3 Smart fabrics can be used in ...
   a engineering.
   b sports.
   c art.
4 The dress made from lights is an example of ...
   a eco-clothing.
   b a design that uses electronics.
   c how to generate electricity from clothes.
5 What do the students think about the dress made of lights?
   a It's very useful.
   b It will become popular in the future.
   c It's not very useful.

8 Look at these sentences. What do you think the words/phrases in bold mean? Match them to the definitions (a–e).

1 I've been looking for an interesting topic, but **to be honest**, I've found nothing in the library.
2 Local workshops are **set up** so that people can earn a salary.
3 And eco-friendly clothing can help protect the environment, too, **apparently**.
4 Some scientists are working on fabrics that can kill bacteria, or **regulate** body temperature.
5 There are fabrics that can help reduce muscle **aches** or prevent us from getting ill.

a started
b control
c to tell the truth
d a small, but continuous pain
e this is what I read

POST-LISTENING

EXPLANATION

Auxiliary verbs for emphasis

In fluent speech, we usually contract auxiliary verbs (*am* ➜ *'m*, *have* ➜ *'ve*, etc.). However, if we want to emphasize a point, we can use the full form. We stress this word.

> That's interesting.
> That _is_ interesting. (= emphasizing that this is interesting)

We can add *do* or *does* to a positive sentence to emphasize our point.

> I like it.
> I _do_ like it. (= emphasizing that I like something)

9 🔊 **8.3** Listen to the sentence pairs below. Which word is stressed in each sentence?

1 **a** That's interesting.
   b That is interesting.
2 **a** I've been reading about fashion in the future.
   b I have been reading about fashion in the future.
3 **a** I agree that it's not very practical.
   b I do agree that it's not very practical.
4 **a** I think it'll be interesting.
   b I do think it'll be interesting.

10 Practice saying the sentence pairs.

11 Change the sentences below to focus on the words in bold by adding *do* or *does*.

1 I **believe** they can be used to make sports clothing.
2 It **seems** we have a lot of ideas for the future of fashion.
3 I **agree**.
4 I **like** the idea of clothes that help people with health problems.
5 She **buys** a lot of clothes.

DISCUSSION

12 Work in pairs and discuss the questions below.

1 What do you think the fashion of the future will be like?
2 Do you always buy the latest fashions? Why/Why not?
3 Why is it important for some people to be fashionable?

⊙ LANGUAGE DEVELOPMENT

IDIOMS AND FIXED EXPRESSIONS

Idioms are fixed expressions that are often used in spoken English. An idiom doesn't always have a literal meaning. It has a meaning than can't easily be understood from looking at its individual words. We need to look at the whole expression.

I see what you mean,
(= I understand. We are not really talking about 'seeing'.)

1 Look at the extracts below. What do you think is the meaning of the expressions in bold?

   1 I've been looking for an interesting topic, but to be honest, I've found nothing in the library. Can you **give me a hand**?

   2 I've been reading about fashion in the future, new designs, interesting new technology, **and all that**.

   3 **As far as I'm concerned**, a dress made from lights is useless.

   4 I'm not **mad about** that idea, to be honest.

   5 Anyway, **at long last**, it seems we have some ideas for the future of fashion.

   6 **Adam:**   So, in the future, we could use this fabric to charge our mobile phones, our cameras, right?
     Clara: Well, **as long as** you keep moving, yes!

   7 I don't think there are many people **dying to** wear a dress made of lights. It sounds like someone designed it **just for the fun of it**.

2 Match the phrases in bold in Exercise 1 with the synonyms below.

   a in my opinion
   b finally, after a long time
   c for pleasure, for a joke
   d enthusiastic about
   e and so on, etc.
   f help me
   g extremely eager to
   h if

TALKING ABOUT THE FUTURE

3 Look at the sentences below. Underline the structures used to talk about the future.

1 It's about future fabrics and how they <u>are going to be</u> used.
2 We will use this fabric to charge our mobile phones, our cameras or other small devices as we walk.
3 We are playing against the other team next month.
4 Maybe someone else will take this idea and create something new.
5 She is leaving for New York tomorrow night.
6 She is going to have a wonderful holiday.

4 Read the conversations below. Match the future forms in bold with their meanings (a–d).

a events that we have planned and intend to do
b timetables and schedules
c predictions based on our knowledge and experience
d a decision made at the time of speaking

1 **A:** Shall I take the umbrella with me?
   B: I think so. Just look at the sky. I think it**'s going to rain**.
2 **A:** What time do you arrive?
   B: The train **arrives** in London at 3.15 pm.
3 **A:** We **are having** a study session before the finals. Do you want to join us?
   B: That would be great. I need some help with the assignment.
   A: No problem. Sashem can help you.
   B: That sounds like a good plan. I**'ll be** there at 7.30.

5 Complete the sentences below with the correct form of the verbs in brackets. Sometimes there is more than one possible answer.

1 I _____ (fly) to London tonight – I have a meeting tomorrow morning.
2 The film _____ (start) at 7:30 every evening except Monday.
3 You look bad. You look like you _____ (be) ill.
4 I have a headache. I think I _____ (stay) at home today and not go into work.

PREPARING TO LISTEN

UNDERSTANDING
KEY VOCABULARY

1 Match the words in bold to their definitions (a–h).

1 Aysha's **collection** was presented during the last Fashion Week in Doha.
2 I have always tried to **combine** my culture with fashion.
3 As a teenager, I would make my own skirts and scarves. I wanted my designs to be **individual**. They were very **unique** and eventually, people **admired** my clothes, rather than laugh at me.
4 When you look at the summer fashion in New York, the **trend** is always to wear skirts, shorts and sleeveless shirts.
5 My philosophy is to create clothes that are **modest** but at the same time, make women feel **confident**.

a to respect or approve of something
b not showing yourself off
c unusual and special
d a group of things (e.g. designs)
e considered as one thing, not part of a group
f to mix or join things together
g certain about yourself and your abilities
h a general development or fashion

USING YOUR
KNOWLEDGE

2 Work with a partner and discuss the questions below.

1 What comes to your mind when you hear the words 'Muslim fashion'?
2 Do you like the clothes in the photograph? Why/Why not?

WHILE LISTENING

LISTENING FOR
MAIN IDEAS

UNLOCK
ONLINE

3 ◀))8.4 Listen to the first part of the interview. Answer the questions.

1 Who is Aysha Al-Husaini?
2 Where is she from?
3 What is she famous for?

4 ◀))8.5 Listen to the next part. Circle the topics that are mentioned.

1 the *burka* – traditional Muslim clothes for women
2 Aysha's first days at design school
3 Aysha's exams at design school
4 Muslim woman like to be fashionable
5 young Muslim women need cheap, affordable clothes
6 fashions in China and India
7 new designers in Pakistan and Indonesia
8 Aysha's future plans

5 🔊 **8.5** Listen again. Write true (T), false (F) or does not say (DNS) next to the statements below.

1 Aysha grew up in Doha.
2 It can be difficult to buy long-sleeved clothes in New York.
3 She started making clothes when she was a teenager.
4 Most Muslim women wear the *burka*.
5 Aysha's teachers asked her why she didn't design Western styles of clothing.
6 Aysha's designs are for women who like to be modest.
7 Many Muslim women want to wear fashionable clothes.
8 Chinese and Indian designers don't use traditional designs.
9 You can buy Aysha's collection in Malaysia and Singapore.

LISTENING FOR
DETAIL

DISCUSSION

6 Work in small groups. Discuss the questions below.

1 Do you think it's possible to combine fashion with tradition?
2 What are the traditional clothes in your country? Do people often wear them?
3 What are the current fashion trends in your country?
4 Which is more important: to dress in an individual way, or to dress in the same way as everyone else? Why?

CRITICAL THINKING

You are going to do the speaking task below.

> Take part in an interview to find out attitudes towards uniforms and dress codes.

APPLY

1 Many people have to wear a uniform at work or in school. Read the opinions below. Are they for (F) or against (A) wearing uniforms?

   1 I feel more confident in a uniform.
   2 It saves me a lot of time in the morning. I don't have to think about what to wear.
   3 I think it's usually cheaper than buying your own clothes.
   4 I feel strange wearing one. I don't feel myself.
   5 I think wearing a uniform should be optional.
   6 It makes everyone equal, and that means no-one has to feel bad about what they're wearing.

2 Tick the opinions in Exercise 1 you agree with. Then work with a partner. Explain why you agree.

> In a discussion or a debate, we sometimes play 'devil's advocate'. This means deliberately disagreeing with someone, or raising a different point of view.
> We might do this even if we don't really want to disagree. The reason we do this is to make sure that both sides of the argument are discussed.

ANALYZE

3 Notice how speaker B raises another point of view:

   A: I don't like uniforms. Everyone looks the same. We lose our individuality.
   B: OK, but you don't have to look exactly the same as everyone else. For example, you could wear your hair in a different way.

4 Match alternative opinions (a–g) to the opinions (1–7) in Exercise 1.

   a OK, so why don't you plan what to wear the night before?
   b Yes, but not everyone is lucky enough to have comfortable uniforms.
   c But it doesn't matter what you wear, does it? There are lots of other ways to be yourself.
   d Yes, but a lot of people feel more confident in their own clothes.
   e But you can't force people to be equal. Everyone is different.
   f Are you sure? Some people have to buy their own uniform, and it can be very expensive.
   g Yes, but if it was optional, then few people would choose to wear one.

EVALUATE

5 Work with the same partner as in Exercise 2. This time, take turns to say which opinions you agree with. Then discuss the alternative point of view.

SPEAKING

PREPARATION FOR SPEAKING

UNLOCK ONLINE

EXPLANATION

Asking for opinions and checking information

We can ask questions in a direct way or an indirect way. Indirect questions change a question so that it asks someone for a 'yes'/'no' answer. This gives the person the choice to answer it fully or not. This means that indirect questions can be used when we want to be more polite.

Where do you get your ideas from? (= direct question)
<u>Can you tell me</u> where you get your ideas from? (= indirect question)

1 Read extracts (a–f) from Listening 2. Then answer the questions.

a Can you tell me where you get your ideas from?

b How did you feel about growing up in New York?

c Do you think that there is a lot of misunderstanding about Muslim clothes?

d And what do you think Muslim fashion is?

e So are you saying that there is a need for fashionable clothes for Muslim women?

f Many reviewers describe your style as 'traditional chic'. Would you agree with this?

g As I understand it, your designs are popular outside the US, is that right?

1 Which question(s) check if the interviewer understood something correctly?

2 Which question(s) are indirect?

2 Circle the phrase that best completes each question.

A: [1]*Would you say that / What do you think* is the best way to dress for a job interview?

B: I think you should wear a suit and a tie.

A: [2]*Would you say that / How do you feel about* I should wear a suit even if I don't usually wear one?

B: That's right. As I see it, you only have 30 minutes to impress your future boss at the interview. You should look your best. [3]*Don't you agree? / What do you mean?*

A: No. I think my skills are more important than what I look like.

B: [4]*Do you mean that / What's your opinion about* you are going to wear jeans and a T-shirt to your job interview?

A: I think so. The company I want to work for isn't interested in appearances.

FOCUSING ON INFORMATION THAT FOLLOWS

3 🔊 8.6 Listen to extracts 1–6. Underline the focusing phrases that tell the listener that important information is coming next.

1 <u>The thing is that</u> when you say 'Muslim fashion', people in New York think of a Burka.

2 Let me give you an example – when I first started at design school, my teachers would ask me strange questions.

3 As far as I'm concerned, there is much more to fashion than showing your body.

4 My feeling is this – I want to create clothes that are modest but at the same time give women confidence.

5 What I think is that combining 'traditional' with 'chic' is a huge area in fashion.

6 Another thing is that I also receive emails from women in Pakistan, Indonesia, Singapore and Malaysia.

4 Listen again. Notice that there is a short pause after the focusing phrases. Why do you think this is?

5 Work with a partner. Look at the information below. Spend two minutes preparing what you will say. Then have a conversation.

Student A	Student B
• Ask Student B for his/her opinion about buying designer clothes. • Ask Student B to explain his/her opinion. Check if you understood what he/she meant.	You don't like buying designer clothes. Give one or two arguments to support your opinion. Use focusing phrases if possible.

6 Now swap roles. Student A, give a positive opinion about designer clothes. Spend two minutes preparing what you will say. Then have a conversation.

SPEAKING TASK

> Take part in an interview to find out attitudes towards uniforms and
> dress codes.

1 Work in small groups. Discuss the questions below.

1 What is a 'dress code'?
2 Why do some schools, colleges or companies have a dress code?
3 Do you think a dress code or uniform is a good idea or should people
    be allowed to wear whatever they like?

2 Work in groups of four (A, B, C and D). Read your roles and make notes.

Student A: interviewer You are working for a college newspaper and you want to find out what students think about dress codes. Make notes about the questions you want to ask.	**Student B: student** You think that a dress code is a good idea at college and at the workplace. Make notes about your opinion.
Student C: interviewer You are working for a college newspaper and you want to find out what students think about dress codes. Make notes about the questions you want to ask.	**Student D: student** You don't think that a dress code is a good idea. Explain your opinion to the interviewer. Make notes about your opinion.

3 Work with a partner. Students A and B work together, Students C and D work together. Practice the interview.

4 Give each other feedback about your performance.

    1 Were there enough questions? What other questions could you add?
    2 Did the interviewer check information?
    3 Did the student give clear opinions?

5 Work with a different partner. Students A and C work together, Students B and D work together. Do the interview again.

TASK CHECKLIST	✔
Did you clearly ask for opinions?	
Did you check information, where necessary?	
Did you focus on information coming next?	

OBJECTIVES REVIEW

I can ...

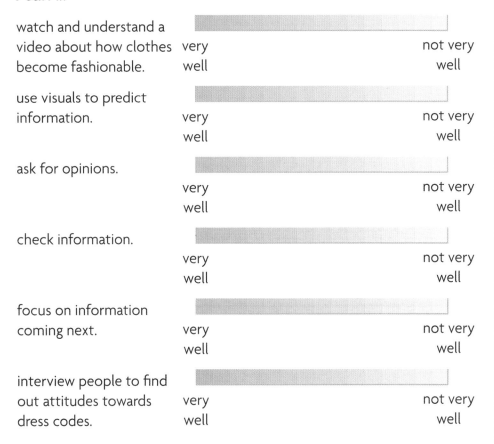

watch and understand a video about how clothes become fashionable.
very well　　　　　　　　not very well

use visuals to predict information.
very well　　　　　　　　not very well

ask for opinions.
very well　　　　　　　　not very well

check information.
very well　　　　　　　　not very well

focus on information coming next.
very well　　　　　　　　not very well

interview people to find out attitudes towards dress codes.
very well　　　　　　　　not very well

WORDLIST

UNIT VOCABULARY	ACADEMIC VOCABULARY
complain (v)	admire (v)
cope with (v)	collection (n)
fabric (n)	combine (v)
local (adv)	conditions (n)
on his own (adv)	confidence (adj)
there's no point (adv)	convert (v)
	design (n)
	focus (v)
	individual (n)
	modest (adj)
	practical (adj)
	products (n)
	trend (n)
	unique (adj)

Watch and listen	Watch and understand a video about the changing economy in China
Listening skills	Identify contrasting viewpoints
Speaking skills	Talk about actions; ask someone to explain more
Speaking task	Debate whether teenagers should have credit cards

UNLOCK YOUR KNOWLEDGE

Work with a partner and discuss the questions below.

1 What can young people do in your country to earn money?

2 How do you save money?

3 Is it worth spending money on things like designer clothes and expensive cars?

WATCH AND LISTEN

PREPARING TO WATCH

UNDERSTANDING
KEY VOCABULARY

1 Choose the answer that best completes each sentence.

1 The _____ situation in this country is very poor. Many people have no money to support themselves.
   a money   **b** economic   **c** educational

2 Many young people in this country are unemployed and have to travel to other countries in _____ jobs.
   a make   **b** succeed   **c** search of

3 Many countries rely on _____ workers to do dangerous jobs.
   a migrant   **b** educated   **c** construction

4 Washing the windows of a very tall building is a _____ experience.
   a relaxing   **b** very frightening   **c** sad

5 Some people take on dangerous jobs because they have to _____ their families.
   a feed   **b** stay away from   **c** spend time with

6 It's not easy to _____ when you don't have education or experience.
   a spend money   **b** be unemployed   **c** make money

7 Many people believe that having a lot of money means _____ .
   a poverty   **b** success   **c** millions

8 It's difficult to _____ when you have a lot of children.
   a save money   **b** spend money   **c** pay tax

2 Look at the photographs and read the extract from the video below. Work in pairs and answer the questions.

> Millions of Chinese move from the countryside to urban areas in search of wealth and success.

1 Why are Chinese people moving into big cities?
2 What kind of jobs can they do in the villages?
3 What kind of jobs can they do in big cities?
4 What problems do they face when they move from a village to a big city?

3 ▶ Watch the video and check your ideas.

WHILE WATCHING

4 ▶ Watch the video and answer the questions below.

1 Why did Sun Feng move from his village to Shanghai?
2 What is his job?
3 Is it an easy job?
4 How often does he visit his family in the village?

5 ▶ Watch the video again. Write true (T) or false (F) next to the statements below.

1 Sun Feng has been living in Shanghai for a year now.
2 There are over 3 million workers in Shanghai.
3 Cleaning skyscraper windows is one of the best paid jobs in the city.
4 Sun Feng is saving money to buy a new car.
5 Sun Feng prefers a simple lifestyle over the rich world of the big cities.
6 Workers visit their families for the Chinese New Year.

DISCUSSION

6 Work in small groups. Discuss the questions below.

1 Are there migrant workers in your country?
2 Where do they usually come from?
3 What kind of jobs do they do?
4 What problems do they face when they come to your country?
5 What are the advantages and disadvantages of using migrant workers?

LISTENING 1

PREPARING TO LISTEN

UNDERSTANDING
KEY VOCABULARY

1 Complete the sentences below with phrases from the box.

> invested all his money   results of this survey   luxury cars
> save money   worth a lot of money   can't afford to
> waste your money   debt to pay   bank loan   wealthy

1 The _____ show that most people spend a lot of money on entertainment.
2 If you want to _____ , you could stop eating out in expensive restaurants.
3 _____ , like a Ferrari or a Rolls Royce can be very expensive.
4 My grandfather _____ in the stock market.
5 I've just paid my college fees. That's why I _____ go out this weekend.
6 Sarah took out a _____ to buy her first house.
7 He used his credit card to go on holidays. Now he has a huge _____ .
8 The Novak family are very _____ . They own several houses in the countryside and drive expensive cars.
9 This car is over 10 years old. It's not _____ any more.
10 If you don't want to _____ , then don't buy cheap clothes. Buy expensive clothes that last a long time.

USING YOUR
KNOWLEDGE

2 Work with a partner. Discuss the questions below.

1 What kind of car do you think millionaires drive?
2 What kind of house do they live in?
3 What kind of clothes do they wear?
4 What would you do if you were a millionaire?

3 Look at the book cover and listen to the introduction of a radio programme about millionaire lifestyles. Then discuss the questions below.

1 Why does the speaker say that the results of the survey were surprising?
2 Can you guess why they were surprising?
3 What does *wealthy* mean?
4 What do you think the rest of the programme will be about?

WHILE LISTENING

4 Work in small groups. Guess which of the behaviours of millionaires below are true.

Millionaires ...
1 drive luxury cars and eat in expensive restaurants.
2 know how much money they spend on food, clothes, etc.
3 live in the same place for a long time.
4 don't spend a lot of money on cars.
5 have successful relationships.
6 borrow money from the bank.
7 are happy with what they have.
8 buy expensive things to feel better.

5 9.2 Listen to the radio programme and check what it says about the ideas in Exercise 4.

6 Work with a partner. What lessons can 'normal' people learn from millionaires?

LISTENING FOR
MAIN IDEAS

UNLOCK
ONLINE

PRONUNCIATION FOR LISTENING

Silent letters

Some English words have letters that are not pronounced aloud. For example, the letter w is not pronounced in *write* and *r* is not always pronounced in *millionaire*.

LISTENING FOR DETAIL

7 Work with a partner. Take turns to say the sentences below.

1 The results of their study were rather **surprising**.
2 Most people think that rich people drive very expensive cars, eat in expensive restaurants, own a **yacht** or live in a big house.
3 According to Holm, most millionaires know **exactly** how much money they have.
4 On the other hand, people who look rich – the people who drive the latest Ferrari, or only wear **designer** clothes – may not actually be rich at all.
5 This means that they don't spend too much, and they don't get into **debt**.
6 There is no **doubt** that it's more difficult to save money if you are single.
7 So what can we learn from the wealthy? The **answer** is surprisingly simple.

8 🔊 **9.3** Listen to the sentences. Pay attention to the pronunciation of the words in bold. Which letters are not pronounced?

9 🔊 **9.2** The sentences below all include <u>false</u> information. Listen to the programme again and correct the sentences.

1 Half of millionaires know how much they spend every year.
2 60% of millionaires have lived in the same house for over 20 years.
3 About 33% of millionaires live in homes which cost $350,000 or less.
4 68% of luxury cars are owned by people who can't afford them.
5 It is easier to save money when you are single.

POST-LISTENING

10 Look at the extracts below. Then answer the questions.

• <u>As John Holm discovered</u>, people who look rich may not actually be rich, because they spend all their money on luxury cars and clothes.
• <u>According to John Holm</u>, half of millionaires have lived in the same house for over 20 years.

1 John Holm is ...
  a the name of the study.
  b the authors of the book.
  c the title of the book.

2 'According to' means ...
  a as a result.
  b because of.
  c as written or stated by.

11 Look at two more extracts and answer the questions.

- <u>The study reveals that</u> 86% of luxury cars are bought by people who can't afford them.
- <u>The study shows that</u> most millionaires have very happy relationships.

1 What does the word *study* refer to in both sentences?
a the research which John Holm did
b John Holm's time at university
c the place where John Holm works

2 The word *reveals* means …
a to hide.
b to advertise.
c to show something that was unknown before.

DISCUSSION

12 Work alone. Decide if you agree with the points made in the programme. Make notes to explain why and think of examples from your own life.

1 Pay close attention to your money.
2 Don't spend more than you have.
3 Don't try to look rich.
4 Pay close attention to your relationships.
5 Be happy.

13 Work in small groups and share your ideas. Decide together which lesson you think is the most important.

◉ LANGUAGE DEVELOPMENT

COLLOCATIONS WITH *PAY, SAVE* AND *MONEY*

1 Add the words from the box to the word maps below.

> spend   attention   someone a visit   make
> time   a fine   earn   energy

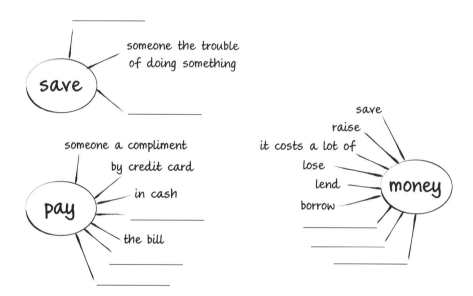

2 Circle the correct words.

1 We *earned / spent* a lot of money on the house. It needed repairs.
2 My company is not *making / paying* any money at the moment. We aren't selling many products.
3 You can *save / pay* a lot of time if you use a computer.
4 She is not *paying / saving* attention to what her teacher is saying.
5 I had to *save / pay* a fine for parking in an illegal place.
6 Hamad *lost / paid* a lot of money by investing in the stock market. He was unlucky.
7 If you switch off the lights when you leave the room, you can *make / save* energy.
8 I *borrowed / lent* money from my mother to buy a new car.
9 I want to *earn / save* money for my wedding, so I have to reduce my spending.
10 After my presentation my friend *paid / lent* me a compliment and said it was very interesting.

CONDITIONAL SENTENCES

EXPLANATION

Conditional sentences

We can use conditional sentences to talk about things which are generally or always true. These are called 'zero conditionals' and they are formed with *if* + present simple.

If people have a lot of money, they are happier.

To talk about things which are possible now or in the future, we can use 'first conditional' sentences. These are formed with *if* + present simple in one clause, and *will* in the other clause.

If I win the lottery, I will buy a new car.

We can also use conditional sentences for advice and suggestions. These are formed with *if you* ... + an imperative.

If you want to be rich, save a lot of money!

3 Look at the extracts (1–4). Answer the questions (a and b) below.

1 If you want to be a millionaire, don't spend a lot on your house.
2 If you don't have to worry about monthly credit-card payments, you are less likely to buy things to improve your mood.
3 If you change houses a lot and live in expensive places, it will be impossible to save money.
4 If you want to comment on these ideas, go to our website.

a Which sentences give advice or make a suggestion?
b Which sentences talk about things that are generally true or possible?

4 The sentences below include mistakes. Add, delete or change one word in each sentence to make them correct.

1 If you want to spend money, you don't buy lots of expensive things.
2 If you have time, listened to this radio programme.
3 If I have money, I always bought new clothes.
4 If you will pay off all your debts, you will be happier.

5 Complete the sentences below with your own ideas. Then work with a partner and discuss your sentences.

1 If you want to save money, ...
2 If you want to be rich, ...
3 If you want to get a better job, ...
4 If you wear expensive clothes, ...

PREPARING TO LISTEN

UNDERSTANDING
KEY VOCABULARY

1 Read the sentences. Match the words in bold with their definitions (a–j).

1 If you have an **opportunity** to work part-time, you should do it.
2 **Statistics** show many students have a bad attitude towards studying.
3 My teacher **encouraged** me to apply to university.
4 I need to **support** my family, so after school, I work part-time in a shop.
5 He has a credit card, but always pays it back late. He has a lot of **financial** problems.
6 She works in a restaurant at the minimum **wage**, but it helps to pay for her textbooks.
7 He was **rewarded** for his work with an increase in salary.
8 She is a hard-working and **responsible** student.
9 My **average** score last semester was very low. I hope to get better marks this semester.
10 My grandfather **dropped out** of school at the age of 16.

a to have the ability to act correctly on your own
b to stop going to classes before finishing a course
c to help someone
d related to money
e money that you receive from your job
f something given in return for good work
g to give someone the confidence to do something
h facts (usually numbers) that show information about something
i the possibility to do something
j an amount calculated by adding all the amounts and then dividing this sum by the number of amounts

USING YOUR
KNOWLEDGE

2 🔊 9.4 Listen to the introduction to a discussion. Work in small groups and look at the question below. Complete the table with arguments for and against the idea.

Should college students be paid for good grades?

for	against

WHILE LISTENING

3 🔊 **9.5** Listen to the discussion and decide whether the following speakers are for (F) or against (A) paying college students for good grades.

1 Dr Michael Burns

2 Mariam Hassan

3 Christine Thorne

4 Listen again and answer the questions below.

1 Why does Dr Burns talk about students working after school and on the weekends?
   a to show that students are hard working
   b to show that working is a good idea for teenagers
   c to explain why students from poor families fail at school

2 According to Mariam, why is paying for grades not a good solution?
   a because it will encourage students to work
   b because it will not solve the real reasons why students drop out
   c because the students don't want to work hard

3 What does Mariam suggest we should spend money on instead of paying for good grades?
   a giving students more support in managing time and stress
   b helping students get a job
   c hiring more teachers

4 What does Dr Burns mean by saying that college students often make the wrong choice?
   a Students are not responsible.
   b Students want to study to get a good job.
   c Students want to make money quickly and don't finish their studies.

5 Who does Christine think we should give money to?
   a parents
   b hard-working teachers
   c creative students

6 Why do some students have a negative attitude to education?
   a Their parents are not interested in education.
   b They don't have time to study.
   c They want to finish college quickly.

LISTENING FOR CONTRASTING VIEWPOINTS

LISTENING FOR DETAIL

UNLOCK ONLINE

POST-LISTENING

5 Look at the extracts below. Answer the questions after each extract.

> I understand that many students drop out from college because of financial problems. However, will paying students really encourage them to continue?

1 The speaker thinks that …
   a we should help students who leave school because they are poor.
   b paying students for good grades will not solve the problem.

> I can see your point, but we have already spent a lot on student services.

2 The speaker thinks …
   a there is no point spending more on student services.
   b student services are a great way to solve the problem.

> I realize that students need encouragement to stay in school, but are we going in the right direction?

3 The speaker thinks paying students for good grades …
   a will encourage them to stay at school.
   b might be a mistake.

6 Look again at the extracts in Exercise 5.

   1 Underline phrases that are used to show that the speaker understands the other person's point of view.
   2 Underline the words used to show that the speaker is going to give a different point of view.

DISCUSSION

7 Make notes on the question below.

> Should college students be paid for good grades?

   1 What is your opinion?
   2 What are your reasons?
   3 Can you give any examples from your own experience to support your reasons?

8 Work in small groups. Take turns to give your opinions, reasons and examples. As a group, decide if students should be paid for good grades or not.

CRITICAL THINKING

1 Work with a partner. Discuss the questions below.

   1 As a child, were you given money by your parents?
   2 If yes, how often did they give you money and why?
   3 Did you ever save any money as a child? What did you do with it?
   4 What do you think about giving children money?

2 🔊 **9.6** Listen to four opinions on the topic of giving children money.
Make notes in the table.

	for	against	reasons
Aseel	✔		help them understand the value of money
Joseph			
Karen			
Robert			

3 Work in small groups. Discuss the questions below.

   1 Which opinions do you agree with? Why?
   2 Which do you disagree with? Why?

4 You want to give your opinion on the topic. Read your roles below and
make notes.

Student A	Student B
• You disagree with Aseel's opinion. • Think of two reasons why you disagree. • Think of a good example to support your reasons.	• You agree with Aseel's opinion. • Think of two reasons that give more support to her opinion. • Think of a good example to support your reasons.

5 Take turns to present your reasons and examples.

SPEAKING

PREPARATION FOR SPEAKING

EXPLANATION

Talking about actions

We can use *-ing* forms in a verb phrase at the start of a sentence to focus on an action. We make this verb phrase the subject of the sentence and put it before the main verb.

*Giving children money **will teach** them how to be responsible.*
*Paying children for housework **is** not a good idea.*

1 Underline the subject in the sentences below.

1 Learning should be about studying new things and improving yourself.
2 Saving money is not easy if you have bills to pay.
3 Reading books about millionaires is not a good way to get rich.
4 Teaching children about money should start at an early age.

2 Rewrite these sentences to focus more on the actions in bold.

1 It is not a good idea to **pay children for housework**.
Paying children for housework is not a good idea.
2 You can encourage children to study if you **pay them**.
3 It's difficult to **learn about money** when you're a child.
4 You can spoil children at an early age if you **give them money**.
5 It is very important to **teach children to save money**.

3 Work with a partner. Complete the sentences with your own ideas.

1 Teaching children about money is ...
2 Giving money to charity is ...
3 Being a millionaire is ...
4 Saving money is ...
5 Spending money on luxury cars is ...
6 Buying designer clothes is ...

UNLƆCK LISTENING AND SPEAKING SKILLS 3

Asking someone to explain more

Sometimes, we need to ask a speaker for more information because something is not clear. We can use phrases like *Can you explain ...?* or *But why shouldn't we ...?* This also allows us to talk more about alternative opinions.

4 🔊 **9.7** Listen to two students discussing whether it's a good idea to give money to children. Circle the phrases they use to ask for reasons.

1 Why do you disagree with ... ?
2 Can you explain why ... ?
3 But what if ... ?
4 Why do you think that ... ?
5 What makes you say that ... ?
6 But why shouldn't we ... ?

5 Work in small groups. Take turns to give opinions on some of the topics below. As you listen to the other students, ask them to explain their reasons. Use phrases from Exercise 4.

- Students shouldn't have to pay for their coursebooks.
- University should be free.
- Children shouldn't have homework.
- We shouldn't pay taxes.

SPEAKING TASK

You are going to participate in a debate on the topic below.

> Should teenagers have credit cards?

PREPARE

1 Read the news story. Discuss the questions below.

> With the financial difficulties faced by many countries around the world, more and more banks are reaching out to teenagers. Many teens are sent advertisements for free credit cards as soon as they become old enough. As a result, many young people get into debt and start their lives owing money to the banks. This situation has started a public debate as to whether young people should be allowed to have credit cards.

1 Do you have a credit card? If yes, at what age did you get it?
2 If you don't have a credit card, would you like to have one? Why?
3 What are some of the problems with credit cards?
4 What is the best age to have your first credit card? Why?

PRACTISE

DISCUSS

2 Work alone. Make a list of the advantages and disadvantages of giving teenagers credit cards.

3 Work in pairs and discuss your ideas.

4 Decide whether you are for or against giving teenagers credit cards. Write examples to support your reasons.

5 Work in small groups. Discuss your opinions on whether teenagers should have credit cards. Give your reasons and examples. As you listen to other students' reasons, ask them to explain their reasons in more detail.

6 Discuss the questions below.

1 Was your point of view strong and well presented?
2 Did you ask your colleagues to give more reasons for their opinion?
3 What could you improve about your arguments?

7 Work in different groups. Make sure that each group has students who agree with the topic and students who disagree with it. Discuss the topic.

8 Present your group's opinions to the class.

TASK CHECKLIST	✔
Did you use collocations with *save*, *pay* and *money* correctly?	
If you used conditional sentences, did you do it correctly?	
Did you talk about actions clearly?	
If you didn't understand someone's opinion, did you ask them to explain more?	

OBJECTIVES REVIEW

I can ...

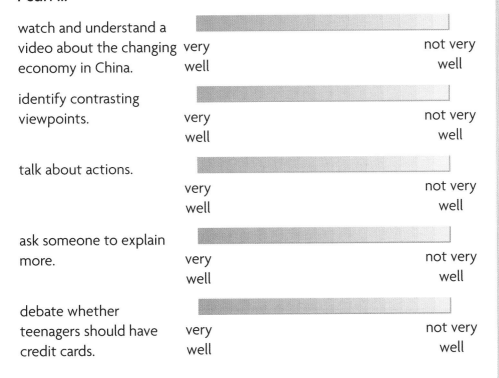

watch and understand a video about the changing economy in China.

very well — not very well

identify contrasting viewpoints.

very well — not very well

talk about actions.

very well — not very well

ask someone to explain more.

very well — not very well

debate whether teenagers should have credit cards.

very well — not very well

WORDLIST

UNIT VOCABULARY		ACADEMIC VOCABULARY	
average (n)	opportunity (n)	borrow money (v)	raise money (v)
bank loan (n)	pay off (v)	cost a lot of money (v)	save energy (v)
can't afford to (v)	results (n)	earn money (v)	save someone the trouble of doing something (v)
continue (v)	reward (n)	lend money (v)	
debt (n)	save money (v)	pay a bill (v)	save time (v)
drop out (v)	statistics (n)	pay a fine (v)	spend money (v)
economic (adj)	success (n)	pay attention (v)	
encourage (v)	support (v)	pay in cash (v)	
financial (n)	wage (n)	pay someone a compliment (v)	
invest (v)	wealthy (adj)	pay someone a visit (v)	
lose money (v)	worth a lot of money (adj)		
luxury (adj)			
make money (v)			

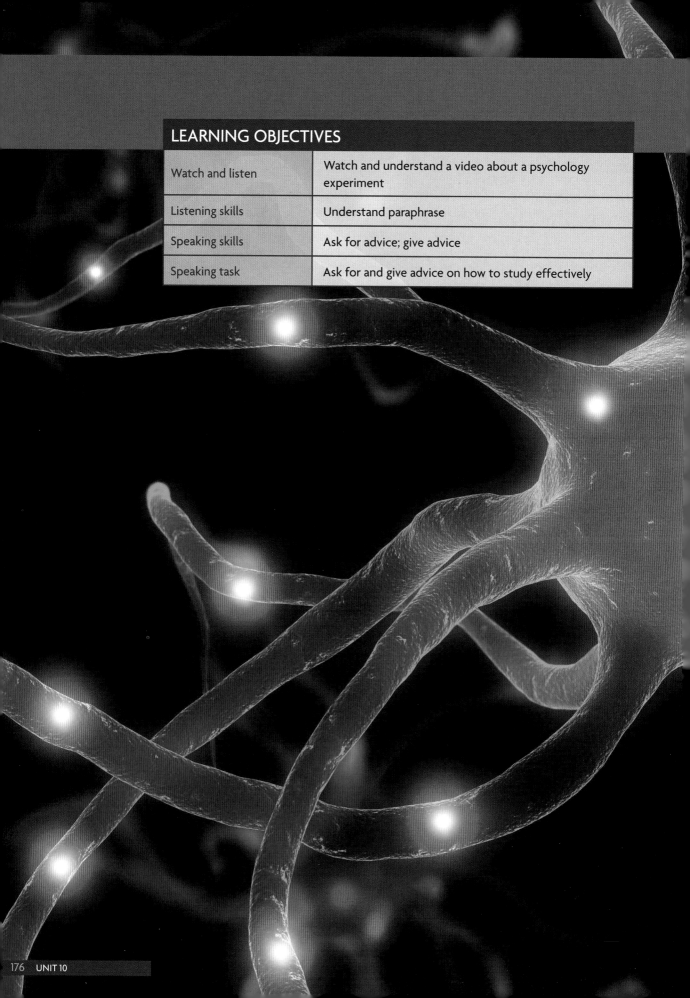

LEARNING OBJECTIVES

Watch and listen	Watch and understand a video about a psychology experiment
Listening skills	Understand paraphrase
Speaking skills	Ask for advice; give advice
Speaking task	Ask for and give advice on how to study effectively

UNL⌀CK YOUR KNOWLEDGE

Work with a partner and discuss the questions below.

1 What's the difference between the *mind* and the *brain*?
2 Is it possible to exercise your brain? How?
3 What things do people do to keep their minds active?

WATCH AND LISTEN

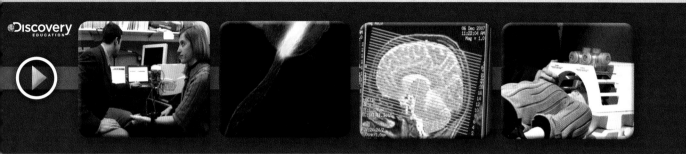

BEFORE WATCHING

1 Complete the sentences below with the words from the box.

> experiment   respond   burned   seem to
> painkiller   ability   occur   alter

1 The student agreed to take part in the _____ to investigate how we learn.
2 The study found out that men and women _____ to pain in a different way.
3 She spilled hot coffee and _____ her arm.
4 These pills _____ work very quickly. I already feel better.
5 This is a powerful _____ . It will stop the pain within one hour.
6 The scientists are testing the _____ of the human brain to reduce pain without using any medicine.
7 This disease can _____ while the brain is still developing.
8 Music can _____ the way we feel.

2 Answer the questions below.

1 What is the placebo effect? Have you heard about it before?
2 Is it possible for people to get better even if they don't take real medicine?
3 What other things besides medicine make sick people feel better?

3 ▶ Watch the video and check your ideas.

WHILE WATCHING

4 ▶ Watch again. Circle the events which happen in the video.

1 A very hot metal plate is placed on Kate's arm.
2 Kate has a cup of coffee.
3 Kate enters a scanner.
4 The doctor puts a type of cream on Kate's skin.
5 Kate takes some painkillers.
6 Kate feels less pain the second time.

5 Work in pairs. Answer the questions below.

1 What does the researcher want to prove by doing the experiment?
2 Is the experiment successful?
3 What does this experiment prove?

6 Watch the video again. Write true (T) or false (F) next to the statements below.

1 Kate is a professor of psychology.
2 The professor burns her on her arm.
3 The placebo effect occurs in your brain when you are given real medicine.
4 The placebo effect produces a physical change in the brain.
5 The professor scans Kate's brain to look for the pain centre.
6 The professor puts a regular body cream on her arm instead of painkillers.
7 Kate still feels a lot of pain after the body cream is put on her arm.
8 The experiment shows that the human brain can respond to a placebo.

DISCUSSION

7 Work in small groups. Discuss the questions below.

1 What information from the video did you find interesting?
2 What are the benefits of knowing about the placebo effect?
3 How can the placebo effect be used by doctors?

LISTENING 1

PREPARING TO LISTEN

UNDERSTANDING
KEY VOCABULARY

UNLOCK
ONLINE

1 Match the words in bold with their definitions (a–j).

1 Huda is very **intelligent** and always comes up with great ideas and solutions.

2 Mark is an **ordinary** student. He does not excel at anything special.

3 **Talented** children can do things that average children can't. Some of them can solve mathematical problems at a very early age.

4 She is **extremely** upset about failing the exam. She will have to repeat the whole course next semester.

5 **Based on** my exam results, I was admitted to the best university in the country.

6 Your genes **determine** your eye colour and your height.

7 I can't **function** without a cup of coffee in the morning. I feel sleepy and tired if I don't have one.

8 The Nobel Prize is given to people for **exceptional** achievements in science and arts.

9 How children develop depends on the **environment** in which they grow up, like their family life and the school system.

10 Einstein's **theory** of relativity changed the way scientists understand time and space.

a has abilities and skills
b control or influence
c not different or special
d using information from
e very special
f able to learn things easily
g an explanation about how something works
h be able to work
i very much
j the conditions you live or work in

Leonardo da Vinci

Ludwig von Beethoven

Albert Einstein

Thomas Edison

2 Work in small groups and discuss the questions below.

1　What do you know about the people in the photographs?

2　What is a *genius*?

3　Do you know of any geniuses from modern times?

3 🔊 **10.1** Listen to the introduction to an interview. Answer the questions below.

1　What is the topic of the programme?

　a　How to receive a Nobel prize.

　b　Can you be born a genius?

　c　Famous geniuses in history.

2　Who is Dr Erik Anderson?

　a　a sociologist

　b　a genius

　c　a psychologist

USING YOUR
KNOWLEDGE

WHILE LISTENING

4 🔊 **10.2** Listen to the rest of the interview and answer the questions below.

1　According to Dr Anderson, are the brains of geniuses different from ordinary people?

2　What helps develop your brain?

3　What is the *10,000-Hour Rule*?

4　According to Dr Anderson, what is more important: being born a genius or working hard?

LISTENING FOR
MAIN IDEAS

PRONUNCIATION FOR LISTENING

5 🔊 **10.3** Listen to the short conversations below. Mark the intonation at the end of each question. Write ➚ if it is rising and ➘ if it is falling.

A: Do you think Einstein was a genius? [1] _____
B: I think so.
A: What is he most remembered for? [2] _____
B: The Theory of Relativity, I think.

A: I think that some people are just born geniuses. Do you agree? [3] _____
B: Well, I think that even if you have a talent, you need to work on it.
A: What about children who are talented at a very early age? [4] _____
B: Yes. Surely they must be born with their talent.

6 Answer the questions below.

1 In which questions in Exercise 5 does the speaker want a 'yes/no' answer?
2 Which questions are open-ended questions?
3 Does the intonation in the 'yes/no' questions rise or fall at the end?

7 Work with a partner. Say the questions below. Decide if the question intonation rises or falls at the end.

1 Dr Anderson, what does it mean to be a genius?
2 In what ways are the brains of talented people different from ordinary brains?
3 Some people say that extremely intelligent people are talented in many areas, like music and mathematics. Is that true?
4 Are you saying there is no such thing as a 'genius' brain?
5 What's the 10,000-Hour rule?
6 'Genius is 1% inspiration and 99% perspiration'? Is that what you mean?

8 🔊 **10.4** Listen and check.

9 🔊 **10.2** Listen to the interview again. Write true (T) or false (F) or does not say (DNS) next to the statements below.

1 A genius is someone who sees things in a unique way.
2 The brain of a genius is different from an ordinary person's.
3 Einstein used different parts of his brain.
4 Playing the violin helps to develop creative thinking.
5 Dr Anderson believes that some people are born geniuses.
6 Steve Jobs never took holidays.
7 Studies show that successful people work hard on one thing for many years.
8 Edison believed that genius depends mostly on having good ideas.

POST-LISTENING

> ## Understanding paraphrase
>
> To paraphrase means to explain an idea in different words, often in a simpler and shorter way. When we paraphrase, we can:
>
> - use synonyms.
> - explain complex or scientific vocabulary in our own words.
> - change the sentence structure.

10 Look at the extracts below. Pay attention to the phrases in bold (in sentences 1–3), which signal that the speaker is going to paraphrase. Then answer the questions (a–d) below.

1 Is being a genius determined by our genes or our environment? **In other words**, are people born a genius or do they become a genius?

2 A genius is someone who is exceptional either in their intelligence or creativity. **To put it another way**, a genius is a unique person because he or she can see ordinary things in a new light.

3 The theory says that if you put 10,000 hours into something, you will become an expert. **That is**, success is a direct result of a lot of hard work.

a In extract 1, which idea has a similar meaning to *to be born a genius*?
b In extract 1, which idea has a similar meaning to *become a genius*?
c In extract 2, which word has the same meaning as *unique*?
d In extract 3, which idea has a similar meaning to *a lot of hard work*?

DISCUSSION

11 Work with a partner. Discuss the questions below.

1 What is your description of a genius?
2 Do you personally know anyone who is a 'genius'?
3 Do you think there are any negative sides to being a genius?
4 Are there any things which you are very good at?

COLLOCATIONS WITH *MIND*

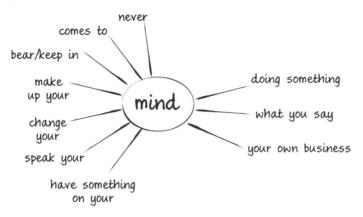

1 Replace the words in bold with phrases from the word map.

1 Who **do you think of** when you hear the word 'genius'?
2 If you have a difficult decision to make, do you **decide** quickly, or does it usually take a long time?
3 When you see someone being treated unfairly, do you usually **keep away** or do you say something?
4 Do you always **say what you think** or do you prefer to keep some things to yourself?
5 What should students **think about** before they choose what subject to study?
6 **Is it a problem** working for no or little money sometimes?

2 Work with a partner. Ask and answer the questions in Exercise 1.

3 Read the dialogues below. Complete the gaps with *mind* collocations.

A: I'm so sorry for being late. I missed the bus.
B: (1)_____ . Let's start the meeting.

A: You look worried. Do you have (2)_____ ?
B: I'm thinking about this research paper. I feel it may be too short.
A: So, what's your research topic?
B: Well, I've (3)_____ since we last talked. I think I will write my paper on the placebo effect instead of intelligence tests.

A: You should really (4)_____ .
B: I realize that now. He looked very upset. I shouldn't have spoken so directly.

LISTENING 2

PREPARING TO LISTEN

1 Read the sentences below and match the words/phrases in bold
(in sentences 1–7) with the definitions (a–i).

1 If you don't use your **muscles**, they become weak and waste away.
2 The best way to keep your mind healthy is to keep it **active**.
3 If you play video games, choose games that **require** you to think and
make **decisions**.
4 The best games are where players have to **solve** puzzles and problems,
rather than just shoot or destroy things.
5 Physical exercise **promotes** blood flow and oxygen levels in your brain,
which **stimulates** brain function.
6 Breakfast is a very important meal because it allows your brain to
work **efficiently**.
7 All physical activity has a **beneficial** effect on your brain.

a choices
b to need something
c busy and doing things
d to make a part of the body do something
e encourages
f working quickly and in an organized way
g the parts of the body which can produce movement
h positive
i find an answer to a problem

2 Work with a partner. Discuss the sentences in Exercise 1. Which do you
think are true?

3 You will hear a conversation between a student and a study counsellor. From the sentences in Exercise 1, and the photographs, guess the answers to the questions below.

    1 What do you think the topic of the conversation is?
       a how to be healthy
       b how to exercise your brain
       c how the brain works
    2 What information will you hear?
       a advice about brain diseases
       b information about different parts of the brain
       c tips on how to keep your brain healthy

4 🔊 **10.5** Listen to the first part of the conversation and check.

WHILE LISTENING

LISTENING FOR
MAIN IDEAS

5 🔊 **10.6** Listen to the conversation and tick which four tips below are mentioned by the study counsellor.

    1 Go to the gym twice a week.
    2 Solve puzzles to keep your brain active.
    3 Watch interesting programmes on TV.
    4 Eat three big meals a day.
    5 Eat fruit for lunch.
    6 Eat food that stimulates your brain.
    7 Make sure you have plenty of sleep.
    8 Make sure you exercise.

6 🔊 10.6 Listen to the conversation again. Write true (T) or false (F) or does not say (DNS) next to the statements below.

1 Puzzles can help you keep your brain active.
2 Listening is an example of an excellent brain exercise.
3 Some video games can help your brain develop.
4 It's recommended to eat a good breakfast.
5 Berries, nuts and fruits contain a lot of Vitamin E.
6 Chocolate doesn't help your brain.
7 Most students need seven hours of sleep at night.
8 Exercising doesn't improve your thinking skills.
9 You should take breaks to exercise when you study for the exams.

POST-LISTENING

7 Look at the sentences below. Underline the phrases used before a summary of the main idea.

1 <u>Overall</u>, if you like to play games, make sure you choose ones that are good for your brain.
2 All in all, you need to learn about foods that are good for your brain.
3 To sum up, you said we should be mentally active, eat food that stimulates brain activity, sleep well and do plenty of exercise.
4 In conclusion, it is important to remember that not everyone can be a genius.
5 Finally, there is plenty of evidence that some foods can help keep our brain healthy.

8 Answer the questions below.

1 Why do we sometimes repeat information when we finish speaking?
2 Is the repeated information a detail or a main idea?

DISCUSSION

9 Work in small groups. Discuss the four tips mentioned in the conversation.

1 Did you learn anything new from the conversation? If so, what?
2 Which piece of advice do you think is the most useful?
3 Which is the least useful?

CRITICAL THINKING

You are going to do the speaking task below.

> Ask for and give advice on how to study effectively and what type of courses to consider.

The theory of multiple intelligences suggests that there are more ways to be intelligent than we usually recognize. For example, people who might be very good at maths might not be very good at art. People who might be very good with visual images might not be good with sounds, etc.

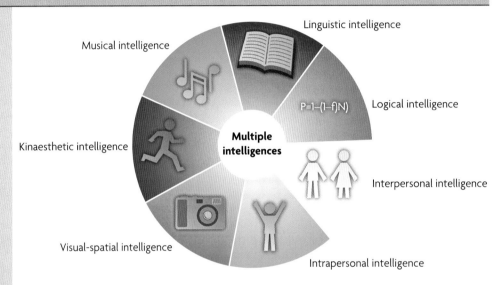

UNDERSTAND

1 Match the intelligences below with their descriptions.

1 Linguistic intelligence	a You like work with other people.
2 Logical intelligence	b You like solving puzzles.
3 Interpersonal intelligence	c You like reading and writing.
4 Intrapersonal intelligence	d You like to sing and listen to music.
5 Visual-spatial intelligence	e You like to think by yourself.
6 Kinaesthetic intelligence	f You like to use videos and pictures.
7 Musical intelligence	g You like to do things with your hands.

APPLY

2 What do you do when you have a problem with a new electronic device? Circle the statements below that are true for you.

a I read the instruction manual for this device.

b I ask friend for help.

c I search for a video to see how it can be solved.

d I spend time thinking about it.

e I work it out by trying different solutions.

f I listen to music while I fix the problem.

g I open the device to see how it works.

3 Work with a partner. Compare your answers, then match the actions (a–g) in Exercise 2 with the intelligences in Exercise 1.

4 Work with a partner. Discuss the intelligences that people might need in the jobs below.

1 lawyer
2 businessman
3 designer
4 movie director
5 engineer
6 chef

5 Work in small groups. Discuss the questions below.

1 Which of the intelligences do you think you have?
2 Which of the intelligences do you think are your weakest?
3 How does this affect the way you like to study English?
4 How does this affect the kind of courses that you choose to study?

EVALUATE

SPEAKING

PREPARATION FOR SPEAKING

ASKING FOR ADVICE

UNL🔒CK
ONLINE

1 🔊 **10.7** Listen to the sentences below. Underline phrases that are used to ask for advice.

1 <u>What advice do you have for</u> students who don't like puzzles?
2 So what can we do to keep our brains healthy and active?
3 Many students don't have time to eat breakfast in the morning. What do you suggest for this?
4 Do you think we ought to eat more chocolate?
5 What should we do when we feel tired?

2 Listen again. What is the intonation at the end of each question? Write ↗ if it is rising and ↘ if it is falling.

3 Work with a partner. Ask and answer the questions below.

1 What advice do you have for students who want to improve their listening skills?
2 What can I do to learn new vocabulary?
3 What do you suggest for meeting people who also want to study English?
4 Do you think I ought to study English every day?
5 What should I do if I don't feel confident about my speaking?

Giving advice

We can use modal verbs for giving advice.

Would, *should* and *ought to* can be used when we are sure about our advice.

> If I were you, I **would** get more sleep.
> You **should/ought to** get more sleep.

We can use *might* or *could* if we don't want to sound so sure.

> It **might** be a good idea to get more sleep.

4 🔊 10.8 Listen to the sentences below. Underline phrases used to give advice.

1 <u>If I were you, I'd</u> read.
2 Make sure that you eat at least one piece of fruit before you leave home in the morning.
3 It would be a good idea to include these foods in your everyday diet.
4 It might be good to eat some chocolate, but make sure it's dark chocolate not just a regular chocolate bar.
5 You should get enough sleep.
6 You ought to sleep around eight hours.

5 Listen again. Circle the stressed words in each underlined phrase in Exercise 4.

6 Work with a partner. You have been asked to give advice to a foreign student who is coming to study in your country. Complete the advice below.

1 If I were you, I'd …
2 You should …
3 It might be a good idea to …
4 You could …
5 You definitely ought to …
6 Make sure you …

7 Work in small groups and compare your ideas.

UNLOCK LISTENING AND SPEAKING SKILLS 3

SPEAKING TASK

You are going to participate in a role-play on the topic below.

> Ask for and give advice on how to study effectively and what type of courses to consider.

1 Look at the intelligence types below. Think about your own learning styles. Which are your strongest intelligences?

1 Interpersonal intelligence
2 Linguistic intelligence
3 Logical intelligence
4 Visual-spatial intelligence
5 Intrapersonal intelligence
6 Kinaesthetic intelligence
7 Musical intelligence

2 Work with a partner. Discuss your ideas. Give examples of things you like to do and the way you like to study that correspond with your strongest intelligences.

3 Work with a partner. Read your roles and make notes on what you will say.

Student A: you are a student	Student B: you are a counsellor
• You are going to talk to a student counsellor about improving your English. • Tell the counsellor about your strengths and weaknesses, and what strategies you should use to improve your English. • Ask about what jobs you should consider in the future.	• Listen to the student and ask for clarification if needed. • Tell the student what you would do if you were in his or her position. • What type of intelligences do you think the student has?

4 Practice your role-play.

5 Now change roles. Student A should be the counsellor. Repeat the discussion.

TASK CHECKLIST	✔
Did you listen clearly to each other?	
Did you ask for advice using appropriate intonation?	
Did you check whether you understood the other speaker?	
Did you use conditional sentences to give advice?	

OBJECTIVES REVIEW

I can ...

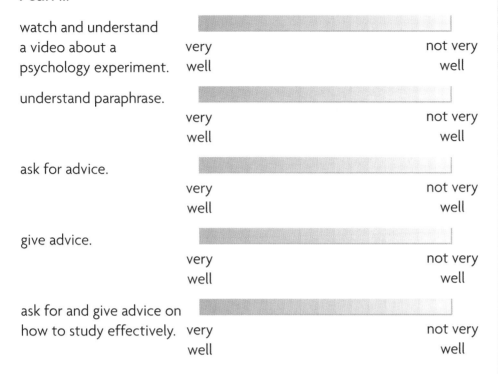

watch and understand
a video about a
psychology experiment.

very well / not very well

understand paraphrase.

very well / not very well

ask for advice.

very well / not very well

give advice.

very well / not very well

ask for and give advice on
how to study effectively.

very well / not very well

WORDLIST

UNIT VOCABULARY		ACADEMIC VOCABULARY
ability (n)	muscle (n)	bear/keep in mind (v)
active (adj)	occur (v)	change your mind (v)
alter (v)	ordinary (adj)	comes to mind (v)
based on (v)	promote (v)	have something on your mind (v)
determine (v)	require (v)	make up your mind (v)
effect (n)	respond (v)	mind doing something (v)
efficiently (adj)	rules (n)	mind what you say (v)
exceptional (adj)	seem to (v)	mind your own business (v)
experiment (n)	solve (v)	speak your mind (v)
extremely (adj)	talented (adj)	
function (v)	theory (n)	
intelligent (adj)	unique (adj)	

GLOSSARY

Vocabulary	Pronunciation	Part of speech	Definition
UNIT 1			
abandon	/əˈbændən/	(v)	to leave someone or something somewhere, sometimes not returning to get them
abuse	/əˈbjuːs/	(n)	cruel, violent, or unfair treatment of someone
analyze	/ˈænəlaɪz/	(v)	to examine the details of something carefully, in order to understand or explain it
benefit	/ˈbenɪfɪt/	(v)	to be helped by something or to help someone
communicate	/kəˈmjuːnɪkeɪt/	(v)	to share information with others by speaking, writing, moving your body or using other signals
conditions	/kənˈdɪʃənz/	(n)	the physical situation that someone/thing is in and affected by
conservation	/kɒntsəˈveɪʃən/	(n)	the protection of nature
convince	/kənˈvɪnts/	(v)	to persuade someone or make them certain
cruel	/ˈkruːəl/	(adj)	extremely unkind and unpleasant and causing pain to people or animals intentionally
debate	/dɪˈbeɪt/	(v)	to discuss a subject in a formal way
domestic	/dəˈmestɪk/	(adj)	belonging or relating to the home, house or family
emergency	/ɪˈmɜːdʒəntsi/	(n)	a serious or dangerous situation that needs immediate action
environment	/ɪnˈvaɪərənmənt/	(n)	the air, land and water where people, animals and plants live
feed	/fiːd/	(v)	to give food to a person, group or animal
harmless	/ˈhɑːmləs/	(adj)	not able or not likely to cause harm
herd	/hɜːd/	(n)	a large group of animals such as cows that live and eat together
humane	/hjuːˈmeɪn/	(adj)	kind, especially towards people or animals that are suffering
involve	/ɪnˈvɒlv/	(v)	to affect or include someone or something in an activity
issue	/ˈɪʃuː/	(n)	a subject or problem which people are thinking and talking about
poisonous	/ˈpɔɪzənəs/	(adj)	very harmful and able to cause illness or death
protect	/prəˈtekt/	(v)	to keep someone or something safe from something dangerous or bad
realize	/ˈrɪəlaɪz/	(v)	to understand a situation, sometimes suddenly
result	/rɪˈzʌlt/	(n)	the information you get from something such as an experiment or test
savannah	/səˈvænə/	(n)	a large flat area of land covered with grass, usually with few trees, which is found in hot countries, especially in Africa
search for	/sɜːtʃ fɔː/	(v)	to try to find someone or something
sedate	/sɪˈdeɪt/	(v)	to give a person or animal a drug to make them feel calm
specialization	/speʃəlaɪˈzeɪʃən/	(n)	a particular area of knowledge
suffer	/ˈsʌfə/	(v)	to experience pain or unpleasant emotions
survive	/səˈvaɪv/	(v)	to continue to live or exist, especially after almost dying or being destroyed
take care of	/teɪk keə ɒv/	(v)	to look after someone or something
treat	/triːt/	(v)	to give medical care to someone for an illness or injury
wildlife	/ˈwaɪldlaɪf/	(n)	animals and plants which grow in natural conditions
zoology	/zuˈɒlədʒi/	(n)	the scientific study of animals and how they behave

Vocabulary	Pronunciation	Part of speech	Definition
UNIT 2			
adapt	/ə'dæpt/	(v)	to change your behaviour so that it is suitable for a new situation
affect	/ə'fekt/	(v)	to have an influence on someone or something, or to cause them to change
alive	/ə'laɪv/	(adj)	living, not dead
anniversary	/ænɪ'vɜːsəri/	(n)	the day on which an important event happened in a previous year
anthropology	/ænθrə'pɒlədʒi/	(n)	the scientific study of human development and society or different societies
behaviour	/bɪ'heɪvjə/	(n)	the way that you behave
die out	/daɪ aʊt/	(v)	to become more and more rare and then disappear completely
event	/ɪ'vent/	(n)	a race, party, competition, etc. that has been organized for a particular time
generation	/dʒenə'reɪʃən/	(n)	all the people in a society or family who are approximately the same age
global	/'gləʊbəl/	(adj)	relating to the whole world
identity	/aɪ'dentəti/	(n)	who someone is and what makes them different from others
interact	/ɪntər'ækt/	(v)	to talk and do things with other people
invention	/ɪn'venʃən/	(n)	something which has been designed or created for the first time, or the act of creating or designing something
multicultural	/mʌlti'kʌltʃərəl/	(adj)	including people of different races and religions
privacy	/'prɪvəsi/	(n)	the right to be alone and do things without other people seeing or hearing you
rule	/ruːl/	(n)	an official instruction about what you must or must not do
share	/ʃeə/	(v)	to have or use something at the same time as someone else
show off	/ʃəʊ'ɒf/	(v)	to try to make people admire your abilities or achievements in a way which other people find annoying
social networking	/'səʊʃəl 'netwɜːkɪŋ/	(n)	using websites to meet people and talk to them
trend	/trend/	(n)	a general development or change in a situation or in the way that people are behaving
upload	/ʌp'ləʊd/	(v)	to send a computer program or a document electronically from your computer, using the Internet
UNIT 3			
ancient	/'eɪntʃənt/	(adj)	from a long time ago
bury	/'beri/	(v)	to put something into a hole in the ground and cover it
conquer	/'kɒŋkə/	(v)	to take control of a country or to defeat people by war
crucial	/'kruːʃəl/	(adj)	extremely important or necessary
defence	/dɪ'fents/	(n)	protection or support against attack, criticism or infection
discover	/dɪ'skʌvə/	(v)	to find out something or to find a place or an object, especially for the first time
find	/faɪnd/	(n)	a good or valuable thing that has been discovered but was not known about before
to found something	/tə faʊnd 'sʌmθɪŋ/	(v)	to bring something into existence
hieroglyph	/'haɪərəʊɡlɪf/	(n)	a picture or symbol that represents a word, used in some writing systems, such as the one used in ancient Egypt

Vocabulary	Pronunciation	Part of speech	Definition
large	/lɑːdʒ/	(adj)	big in size or amount
major	/ˈmeɪdʒə/	(adj)	more important, bigger or more serious than others of the same type
object	/ˈɒbdʒekt/	(n)	a thing that you can see or touch but that is usually not alive
period	/ˈpɪəriəd/	(n)	a length of time
protect	/prəˈtekt/	(v)	to keep someone or something safe from something dangerous or bad
risky	/ˈrɪski/	(adj)	dangerous because something bad might happen
rule	/ruːl/	(v)	to be in control of somewhere, usually a country
significant	/sɪgˈnɪfɪkənt/	(adj)	important or noticeable
statue	/ˈstætʃuː/	(n)	a model that looks like a person or animal, usually made from stone or metal
tomb	/tuːm/	(n)	a place where a dead person is buried, usually with a stone structure
treasure	/ˈtreʒə/	(n)	very valuable things, usually in the form of a store of precious metals, precious stones or money
vital	/ˈvaɪtəl/	(adj)	necessary or extremely important
weapon	/ˈwepən/	(n)	any object used in fighting or war, such as a gun, bomb, sword, etc.
UNIT 4			
achieve	/əˈtʃiːv/	(v)	to succeed in doing something good, usually by working hard
afraid/scared	/əˈfreɪd/skeəd/	(adj)	frightened
attitude	/ˈætɪtʃuːd/	(n)	how you think or feel about something, and how this makes you behave
avoid	/əˈvɔɪd/	(v)	to stay away from a person, place, situation, etc.
break the law	/breɪk ðə lɔː/	(ph)	to do something illegal
challenge	/ˈtʃælɪndʒ/	(v)	something that is difficult and that tests someone's ability or determination
compare	/kəmˈpeə/	(v)	to examine the ways in which two people or things are different
complete	/kəmˈpliːt/	(v)	to finish doing or making something
concentrate	/ˈkɒntsəntreɪt/	(v)	to think very carefully about something you are doing and nothing else
consist of	/kənˈsɪst ɒv/	(v)	to be made of something
control	/kənˈtrəʊl/	(v)	to make someone or something do what you want
convenience	/kənˈviːniənts/	(n)	the quality of being convenient
crash	/kræʃ/	(v)	to have an accident in a vehicle
cure	/kjʊə/	(v)	to make someone with an illness healthy again
damaged	/ˈdæmɪdʒd/	(adj)	harmed or spoilt
design	/dɪˈzaɪn/	(v)	to draw or plan something before making it
efficiency	/ɪˈfɪʃəntsi/	(n)	when someone or something uses time and energy well, without wasting any
engine	/ˈendʒɪn/	(n)	the part of a vehicle that uses energy from oil, electricity or steam to make it move
experience	/ɪkˈspɪəriənts/	(n)	knowledge that you get from doing a job, or from doing, seeing, or feeling something
fine	/faɪn/	(n)	an amount of money that you must pay for breaking a rule or law
goal	/gəʊl/	(n)	an aim or purpose
hit	/hɪt/	(v)	to touch someone or something quickly and with force, usually causing injury or damage

Vocabulary	Pronunciation	Part of speech	Definition
injure	/ˈɪndʒə/	(v)	to hurt a person, animal or part of your body
method	/ˈmeθəd/	(n)	a way of doing something, often one that involves a system or plan
network	/ˈnetwɜːk/	(n)	a system of parts connected together
old-fashioned	/ˌəʊldˈfæʃənd/	(adj)	not modern
positive	/ˈpɒzətɪv/	(adj)	feeling enthusiastic and happy about your life and your future
prevent	/prɪˈvent/	(v)	to stop something from happening or someone from doing something
relax	/rɪˈlæks/	(v)	to become happy and comfortable because nothing is worrying you, or to make someone do this
respect	/rɪˈspekt/	(v)	If you respect someone's rights, customs, wishes, etc. you accept their importance and are careful not to do anything they would not want.
safety	/ˈseɪfti/	(n)	the state of being safe, or a place or situation where someone or something is safe
speed	/spiːd/	(n)	how fast something moves or happens
turbulence	/ˈtɜːbjələnts/	(n)	strong sudden movements within air or water
UNIT 5			
affordable	/əˈfɔːdəbəl/	(adj)	not expensive
benefit	/ˈbenɪfɪt/	(v)	to be helped by something or to help someone
climate change	/ˈklaɪmət tʃeɪndʒ/	(n)	the way the Earth's weather is changing
disadvantage	/dɪsədˈvɑːntɪdʒ/	(n)	something which makes a situation more difficult, or makes you less likely to succeed
disaster	/dɪˈzɑːstə/	(n)	something that causes great harm or damage
environmentally friendly	/ɪnvaɪərənmentəli ˈfrendli/	(adj)	not harmful to the environment
fossil fuel	/ˈfɒsəl ˈfjuːəl/	(n)	a fuel such as coal or oil that is obtained from under the ground
greenhouse	/ˈgriːnhaʊs/	(n)	a building made of glass for growing plants in
heat	/hiːt/	(n)	the quality of being hot or warm, or the temperature of something
long-term	/lɒŋˈtɜːm/	(adj)	continuing a long time into the future
opponent	/əˈpəʊnənt/	(n)	someone who disagrees with an action or belief and tries to change it
pollute	/pəˈluːt/	(v)	to make water, air, soil, etc. dirty or harmful
provide	/prəˈvaɪd/	(v)	to give someone something that they need
reduce	/rɪˈdʒuːs/	(v)	to make something less
region	/ˈriːdʒən/	(n)	a particular area in a country or the world
remove	/rɪˈmuːv/	(v)	to take something away
risk	/rɪsk/	(n)	the possibility of something bad happening
solution	/səˈluːʃən/	(n)	the answer to a problem
spread	/spred/	(v)	to cover or reach a wide area
steam	/stiːm/	(n)	the hot gas that is produced when water boils
uncertain	/ʌnˈsɜːtən/	(adj)	not completely sure
UNIT 6			
break down	/breɪkˈdaʊn/	(v)	If a machine or vehicle breaks down, it stops working.
bring up	/brɪŋ ʌp/	(v)	to care for a child until it is an adult, often giving it particular beliefs
choice	/tʃɔɪs/	(n)	a person or thing that has been chosen or that can be chosen

Vocabulary	Pronunciation	Part of speech	Definition
doubt	/daʊt/	(n)	when you are not certain about something, or do not trust someone or something
gene	/dʒiːn/	(n)	part of the DNA that controls the physical development of a living thing
get on with	/get ɒn wɪð/	(v)	to be able to like or work with someone
get over	/get ˈəʊvə/	(v)	to get better after an illness
give up	/gɪv ʌp/	(v)	If you give up a habit such as smoking, or give up something unhealthy such as alcohol, you stop doing it or having it.
go on for	/gəʊ ɒn fɔː/	(v)	to happen
go out	/gəʊ aʊt/	(v)	to leave a place in order to go somewhere else
goal	/gəʊl/	(n)	an aim or purpose
habit	/ˈhæbɪt/	(n)	something that you do often and regularly, almost without knowing that you are doing it
improve	/ɪmˈpruːv/	(v)	to get better or to make something better
increase	/ɪnˈkriːs/	(v)	to get bigger or to make something bigger in amount or size
ingredient	/ɪnˈgriːdiənt/	(n)	one of the parts of something successful
lifestyle	/ˈlaɪfstaɪl/	(n)	the way that you live
make st. out	/meɪk aʊt/	(v)	to be able to see, hear or understand something
matter	/ˈmætə/	(v)	to be important, or to affect what happens
natural	/ˈnætʃərəl/	(adj)	Something that is natural exists or happens because of nature, not because it was made or done by people.
overweight	/əʊvəˈweɪt/	(adj)	too heavy or too fat
product	/ˈprɒdʌkt/	(n)	something that is made or grown to be sold
prove	/pruːv/	(v)	to show that something is true
regularly	/ˈregjələli/	(adv)	often
scent	/sent/	(n)	a pleasant smell
take over	/teɪk ˈəʊvə/	(v)	to get control of something
treatment	/ˈtriːtmənt/	(n)	the use of drugs, exercises, etc. to cure a person of an illness or injury
well-being	/welˈbiːɪŋ/	(n)	the state of feeling healthy and happy
work out	/wɜːkˈaʊt/	(v)	to exercise in order to improve the strength or appearance of your body

UNIT 7

achievement	/əˈtʃiːvmənt/	(n)	something very good and difficult that you have succeeded in doing
allow	/əˈlaʊ/	(v)	to give permission for someone to do something, or to not prevent something from happening
available	/əˈveɪləbəl/	(adj)	If something is available, you can use it or get it.
beyond	/biˈjɒnd/	(adv)	further away in the distance (than something)
common	/ˈkɒmən/	(adj)	happening often or existing in large numbers
contain	/kənˈteɪn/	(v)	If one thing contains another, it has it inside it.
delay	/dɪˈleɪ/	(n)	when you have to wait longer than expected for something to happen, or the time that you have to wait
design	/dɪˈzaɪn/	(v)	to draw or plan something before making it
develop	/dɪˈveləp/	(v)	to make something new such as a product
device	/dɪˈvaɪs/	(n)	a piece of equipment that is used for a particular purpose

Vocabulary	Pronunciation	Part of speech	Definition
diagram	/ˈdaɪəgræm/	(n)	a simple picture showing what something looks like or explaining something
efficiency	/ɪˈfɪʃəntsi/	(n)	when someone or something uses time and energy well, without wasting any
fix	/fɪks/	(v)	to repair something
ink	/ɪŋk/	(n)	a coloured liquid that you use for writing, printing, or drawing
install	/ɪnˈstɔːl/	(v)	to put a computer program onto a computer so that the computer can use it
instruction	/ɪnˈstrʌkʃən/	(n)	advice and information about how to do or use something
lift	/lɪft/	(v)	to move something from a lower to a higher position
make a (big) difference	/meɪk ə ˈdɪfərənts/	(ph)	to improve a situation (a lot)
make a discovery	/meɪk ə dɪˈskʌvəri/	(ph)	to find information, a place, or an object, especially for the first time
make a mistake	/meɪk ə mɪˈsteɪk/	(ph)	to be wrong about or to fail to recognize something or someone
make sure	/meɪk ʃɔː/	(v)	to take action so that you are certain that something happens
phenomenon	/fəˈnɒmɪnən/	(n)	something interesting or unusual that can be felt, seen, etc.
position	/pəˈzɪʃən/	(v)	to put something or someone in a particular place
recommend	/rekəˈmend/	(v)	to say that someone or something is good or suitable for a particular purpose
weapon	/ˈwepən/	(n)	any object used in fighting or war, such as a gun, bomb, sword, etc.
weight	/weɪt/	(n)	the amount that something or someone weighs
UNIT 8			
admire	/ədˈmaɪə/	(v)	to find someone or something attractive and pleasant to look at
collection	/kəˈlekʃən/	(n)	a group of things or people
combine	/kəmˈbaɪn/	(v)	to become mixed or joined, or to mix or join things together
complain	/kəmˈpleɪn/	(v)	to say that something is wrong or that you are annoyed about something
condition	/kənˈdɪʃən/	(n)	the particular state that something or someone is in
confidence	/ˈkɒnfɪdənts/	(n)	when you are certain of your ability to do things well
convert	/kənˈvɜːt/	(v)	to change the appearance, form, or purpose of something
cope with	/kəʊp wɪð/	(v)	to deal successfully with a difficult situation
design	/dɪˈzaɪn/	(n)	a drawing which shows how an object, machine, or building will be made
focus	/ˈfəʊkəs/	(v)	to give a lot of attention to one particular person, subject, or thing.
individual	/ɪndɪˈvɪdʒuəl/	(adj)	considered separately from the other things in a group
local	/ˈləʊkəl/	(adj)	relating to an area near you
modest	/ˈmɒdɪst/	(adj)	not large in size or amount, or not expensive or important
trend	/trend/	(n)	a general development or change in a situation or in the way that people are behaving
unique	/juːˈniːk/	(adj)	different from everyone and everything else
UNIT 9			
average	/ˈævərɪdʒ/	(adj)	an average number is the number you get by adding two or more amounts together and dividing the total by the number of amounts.
bank loan	/bæŋk ləʊn/	(n)	an amount of money that is borrowed and has to be paid back, usually together with an extra amount of money that you have to pay as a charge for borrowing.

Vocabulary	Pronunciation	Part of speech	Definition
borrow money	/ˈbɒrəʊ ˈmʌni/	(v)	to get or receive money from someone with the intention of giving to back after a period of time
can't afford to	/kɑːnt əˈfɔːd tuː/	(v)	to not be able to buy or do something because you do not have enough money or time
continue	/kənˈtɪnjuː/	(v)	to keep happening, existing or doing something
cost a lot of money	/kɒst ə lɒt ɒv ˈmʌni/	(ph)	expensive to buy
debt	/det/	(n)	an amount of money that you owe someone
drop out	/drɒpˈaʊt/	(ph)	to stop doing something before you have completely finished
earn money	/ɜːn ˈmʌni/	(v)	to receive money as payment for work that you do
economic	/iːkəˈnɒmɪk/	(adj)	relating to trade, industry and money
encourage	/ɪnˈkʌrɪdʒ/	(v)	to make someone more likely to do something, or to make something more likely to happen
financial	/faɪˈnænt ʃəl/	(adj)	relating to money or how money is managed
invest	/ɪnˈvest/	(v)	to give money to a bank, business, etc., or buy something, because you hope to get a profit
lend money	/lend ˈmʌni/	(v)	to give money to someone for a short period of time, expecting it to be given back
lose money	/luːz ˈmʌni/	(v)	to have less money than you had before
make money	/meɪk ˈmʌni/	(v)	to increase the amount of money that you have, generaly thourh work or an activity
opportunity	/ɒpəˈtʃuːnəti/	(n)	a situation in which it is possible for you to do something, or a possibility of doing something
pay a bill	/peɪ ə bɪl/	(ph)	to give money for something that you have used or received
pay a fine	/peɪ ə faɪn/	(ph)	to give an amount of money that has to be paid as a punishment for not obeying a rule or law
pay attention (to sth)	/peɪ əˈtentʃən/	(ph)	to watch, listen to, or think about something carefully
pay in cash	/peɪ ɪn kæʃ/	(ph)	to give money in the form of notes and coins, rather than cheques or credit cards
pay off	/peɪˈɒf/	(v)	to pay back money that you owe
pay someone a visit	/peɪ ˈsʌmwʌn ə ˈvɪzɪt/	(ph)	to visit a person or place, usually for a short time
raise money	/reɪz ˈmʌni/	(ph)	to collect money, often for a cause
result	/rɪˈzʌlt/	(n)	information that you get from something such as an exam, a scientific experiment, or a medical test
reward	/rɪˈwɔːd/	(n)	something good that you get or experience because you have worked hard, behaved well, etc.
save energy	/seɪv ˈenədʒi/	(ph)	to prevent physical and mental activity from being wasted or spent
save money	/seɪv ˈmʌni/	(ph)	to prevent money from being wasted or spent
save someone the trouble of doing something	/seɪv ˈsʌmwʌn ðə ˈtrʌbəl ɒv ˈduːɪŋ ˈsʌmθɪŋ/	(ph)	to help someone by making an action not necessary
save time	/seɪv taɪm/	(v)	to prevent time from being wasted or spent
spend money	/spend ˈmʌni/	(v)	to give money as a payment for something
statistics	/stəˈtɪstɪks/	(n)	a collection of facts in the form of numbers that shows information about something
success	/səkˈses/	(n)	when you achieve what you want to achieve
support	/səˈpɔːt/	(v)	to help someone, often when they are having problems

Vocabulary	Pronunciation	Part of speech	Definition
wage	/weɪdʒ/	(n)	the amount of money a person regularly receives for their job
wealthy	/ˈwelθi/	(adj)	rich
worth a lot of money	/wɜːθ ə lɒt ɒv ˈmʌni/	(ph)	having a high monetary value
UNIT 10			
ability	/əˈbɪləti/	(n)	the physical or mental skill or qualities that you need to do something
active	/ˈæktɪv/	(adj)	doing a lot of things, or moving around a lot
alter	/ˈɔːltə/	(v)	to change, or to make someone or something change
based on	/beɪst ɒn/	(v)	If you base something on facts or ideas, you use those facts or ideas to develop it
bear/keep in mind	/beə/kiːp ɪn maɪnd/	(ph)	to remember a piece of information when you are making a decision or thinking about a matter
change your mind	/tʃeɪndʒ jɔː maɪnd/	(ph)	to change a decision or opinion
comes to mind	/kʌmz tuː maɪnd/	(ph)	remembered or thought of
effect	/ɪˈfekt/	(n)	the result of a particular influence
efficiently	/ɪˈfɪʃəntli/	(adv)	quickly and effectively in an organized way
exceptional	/ɪkˈsepʃənəl/	(adj)	extremely good
experiment	/ɪkˈsperɪmənt/	(n)	a test, especially a scientific one, that you do in order to learn something or to discover whether something is true
extremely	/ɪkˈstriːmli/	(adv)	very, or much more than usual
function	/ˈfʌŋkʃən/	(n)	the purpose of something or the particular responsibility of someone
intelligent	/ɪnˈtelɪdʒənt/	(adj)	showing intelligence, or able to learn and understand things easily
make up your mind	/meɪk ʌp jɔː maɪnd/	(ph)	to decide
muscle	/ˈmʌsəl/	(n)	one of many pieces of tissue in the body that are connected to bones and which produce movement by becoming longer or shorter
occur	/əˈkɜː/	(v)	to happen, often without being planned
ordinary	/ˈɔːdənəri/	(adj)	not special, different, or unusual in any way
promote	/prəˈməʊt/	(v)	to encourage something to happen or develop
require	/rɪˈkwaɪə/	(v)	to need or demand something
respond	/rɪˈspɒnd/	(v)	to say or do something as a reaction to something that has been said or done
rule	/ruːl/	(n)	an official instruction about what you must or must not do
seem to	/siːm tuː/	(v)	to give the effect of being; to be judged to be
solve	/sɒlv/	(v)	to find the answer to something
talented	/ˈtæləntɪd/	(adj)	with talent
theory	/ˈθɪəri/	(n)	an idea or set of ideas that is intended to explain something
unique	/juːˈniːk/	(adj)	unusual and special

UNIT 1

 Wildlife conservation

This is the South African savannah: a huge open area of grassland in the east of the country. Warm air from the Indian Ocean brings plenty of rainfall and a land full of life. Here you will find lions and rhinos, zebras, elephants and giraffes, and a South African gazelle called the springbok, all living in one of the world's great natural wildlife parks.

Wildlife vets like Jana Pretorius work hard to protect South Africa's animal species. Jana moves 6,000 animals across the country each year, taking them back to places where they used to live and helping to increase the population. It is thanks to people like Jana that South Africa leads the world in wildlife conservation, with 10% of the country set aside for the protection of wildlife. Today, Jana and her team have to find, capture, and relocate a male giraffe which is five and a half metres tall.

Jana flies over the savannah in a helicopter, searching for the giraffe. The helicopter flies low over the trees, travelling at 160 km an hour. When Jana finds the giraffe she will have to shoot it with a sedative dart. The sedative is very strong. One teaspoon of it would kill 25 people.

On the ground, Jana's team travel in trucks. It is their job to control the giraffe after Jana has sedated it. This is very dangerous work. It takes Jana an hour to find the giraffe herd. She isolates the tallest male and shoots him with the sedative dart.

The team need to get to the giraffe and keep it in the open. If Jana doesn't give the giraffe the antidote quickly enough, it will die.

Everything goes well. Jana wakes the giraffe up and the team gets the animal on the truck. It will now travel 800 kilometres to its new home, while Jana flies off to her next job.

🔊 **1.1**

Presenter: Hello and welcome to this week's episode of Unicast, a podcast about our students and their lives. Today we have a special guest, Aisha.

Aisha: Hi there!

Presenter: Aisha is a fourth-year veterinary student and she is graduating in three months' time. Can you tell us how it feels to be so close to finishing your degree?

Aisha: It feels fantastic! The last four years have been really hard, but the veterinary school has been everything I hoped for.

Presenter: Did you always want to be a vet?

Aisha: Oh yes, pretty much since I was a child. I grew up in a small village in the mountains just outside Nizwa in Oman, and we've always been surrounded by animals – like cats, dogs, donkeys, goats, horses ... You name it! I even had a pet rabbit!

Presenter: Weren't you ever afraid of all those animals?

Aisha: No, not at all. My parents taught me to love animals. I had to look after the animals when I was a child, so when I graduated from high school, I decided to study Zoology at the university in Muscat.

Presenter: So that was your first degree?

Aisha: Yes, after a BSc in Zoology, I got a job as a veterinary assistant.

Presenter: And what did you do?

Aisha: Well, my job was to help with the animals – clean them, feed them and take care of them. It was an amazing experience and it convinced me to apply to veterinary school. You have to love animals to be a vet.

 1.3

Presenter: And what did you study, exactly?

Aisha: At the veterinary school, there are three types of specialization. The first one is small animals, like cats and dogs. The second one is large animals like camels, horses, cows. And the last one is exotic animals – like snakes. I specialize in small animals.

Presenter: And so what courses do you need to complete to get a veterinary degree?

Aisha: A lot of different courses. In the first two years, we study basic sciences, like Chemistry, Anatomy and Biology. I was shocked in the first year with the amount of material that we were expected to read and understand in a short period of time.

Presenter: And did it get easier?

Aisha: Not really, but we got used to it. In the third year, we did more lab work. It was surprising how often vets need to analyze lab results.

Presenter: And what have you been doing in the last year?

Aisha: In the fourth year, students have to practise working with a real veterinarian. At the moment, I'm working in a vet's clinic. I help examine, diagnose and treat sick animals.

Presenter: And what kind of cases do you deal with, usually?

Aisha: We do get a lot of emergencies. The most common are food poisoning or bites. Many pet owners don't realize that food which is harmless to humans can be dangerous to their pets. For example, chocolate is poisonous to cats and dogs. They can die if they eat it. You should never give your pet human food. We also treat snake bites. That happens a lot.

Presenter: Do you have any tips for students who would like to become vets?

Aisha: Yes. First of all, you should think carefully about if you really want to do this. It's hard work. I start my day at 5.30 a.m. and go to bed late at night. I work most mornings and afternoons at the hospital and then study for my exams in the evening. I would not be able to do this if I didn't love my job. Secondly, before you decide to be a vet, you should try working in a local animal shelter or zoo. It's an excellent experience and it will help you decide whether being a vet is right for you.

Presenter: That's excellent advice. Thank you Aisha. That's it for this episode. Thanks for listening and …

 1.4

Presenter: Hello. Today's debate is on using animals for work.

The oldest domesticated animal is the dog. They protect our houses, look after us, and keep us safe. Other domesticated animals – used for food – include sheep, cows and goats. The first donkeys were used by humans approximately 6,000 years ago in Egypt. Horses were domesticated 5,000 years ago in Europe and Asia. All these animals have been used to help human beings survive, either by providing food or by working for us. Horses, camels, elephants – they have all helped humans explore their land and transport goods from one place to another. But is this fair? What about animal rights? To argue this issue with me today is Amy Johnson, an animal rights activist and writer. To argue against the issue is Dr Jacob Kuryan. Dr Kuryan is a professor of Zoology and a writer of several books on animal welfare. You both have two minutes to introduce your point of view. Amy, would you like to begin?

Amy: Thank you for inviting me to this debate. It's well known that animals have worked side-by-side with humans for thousands of years. In fact, they helped us develop our civilisation and have helped humans survive. Animals, like elephants and horses, were used to build amazing structures, like the pyramids. Yet their hard work and suffering are hardly ever acknowledged. Horses, camels and elephants were used to transport armies and soldiers during wars. But many of these animals died in these wars. And there are other examples. Even now, dogs are used to pull sledges in cold climates and elephants are used for logging. These animals work long hours for very little reward. Humans just use them to their advantage. My main argument is that, in the modern world, there is no longer any need to use animals for work. We have technology that can replace them. It is similar to using children to work in factories. Two hundred years ago, factory owners got rich by using children. Nowadays, people still get rich by using animals to do work for them. The problem is that the animals have no one to represent them and protect their rights. Even though animals work hard for us, they are often abandoned when they get sick or too old to work. They suffer. In short, I strongly believe that using animals for work is an old-fashioned and inhumane practice.

Presenter: Thank you Amy. Dr Kuryan – your introduction, please.

Dr Kuryan: Thank you. It's true that animals have helped our civilisation develop. Camels and horses helped us to carry goods across huge distances. Dogs helped us hunt and protected us from wild animals. I want to argue that in many developing countries, poor people still need animals to survive. These are people who can't afford cars, house alarms or expensive machines. Another point is that without humans, these domesticated animals would not have been able to survive. They need us and we look after them. Not all animal use is abuse. There are many pet owners and animal lovers around the world who work in animal shelters and help animals. There are laws that stop animals suffering. Here's an interesting point – in modern cities, we don't see animals suffering. On the contrary, developed countries spend a lot of money every year on pet food, pet toys, and health care. We even have pet spas where our furry friends can get a massage and first-class treatment for a day. At the same time, there are still millions of children in the world who don't get this kind of treatment. They go without food or clothing. I strongly believe that, in a modern society, people often care more for animals than the poor.

Presenter: Thank you both of you for your arguments! Now, let's hear from our listeners …

🔊 **1.5**

It's often said that it's cruel to use animals for entertainment. However, I would like to argue against this idea. I know that many animal lovers would disagree with me, but let me explain my point of view. First of all, keeping animals in zoos helps protect them. For example, many species such as the giant panda or the snow leopard are endangered. Yet, they are safer in zoos. Another point is that zoos have an important educational role. When I was a child, my father took me to the zoo. I learned about exotic animals and I also learned to care about animals. Modern zoos have improved their conditions. Animals are no longer kept in small cages, zoos have large areas where animals can feel as if they are in their natural habitat. To summarize the main points, zoos help protect animals and educate us. Finally, modern zoos are comfortable, safe places for wild animals. In conclusion, I believe that we should help zoos by visiting, or donating money.

UNIT 2

▶ Japan: customs and traditions

Japan is an island nation made up of a group of islands surrounded by the sea. The island of Japan has a population of just under 130 million people. This population is falling as people age, and fewer and fewer babies are born.

In Japan the average life expectancy is 79 for Japanese men, and Japanese women live even longer with an average age of 86.

On the main island of Honshu is a small town called Toba. Here a two-thousand-year-old tradition is being kept alive by a group of women who are in their eighties. They are ama divers. Ama means a sea person.

Ama are normally women. This is because the Japanese believe that women have more fat in their bodies which helps keep them warm in the cold water. Diving keeps them fit and feeling young.

Many of this generation have been diving since they left school in their teens. The women free dive without tanks of oxygen, but they wear white clothing which is meant to protect the women from shark attacks. The Ama believe sharks don't like the colour white.

Ama divers used to dive for pearls, but due to large pearl farms this practice is now no longer profitable. Ama now dive mainly for seafood.

Meanwhile, all over Japan, people are celebrating the arrival of Spring and the cherry blossom, or 'Sakura'. Cherry blossom is a national symbol of Japan. The flowers are white or pink.

During the spring, there are programmes every day on TV that tell people when the flowers will arrive. When they arrive, everyone in the towns, cities and countryside joins in the celebrations. People go to parks and gardens to look at the flowers. They take lots of photos on their phones and cameras. People eat and drink under the trees, and celebrations carry on well into the night.

🔊 **2.1**

This Sunday on *Book of the Week*, we interview Robert Lee, a well-known anthropologist and the author of *Changing Traditions in the Modern World*. In this programme, we will discuss his love for cultural anthropology, whether traditions are adapting to the modern world or dying out. Join us at 1 p.m.

🔊 **2.2**

Presenter: Welcome to this week's book review. In the studio with me is Dr Robert Lee, Professor of Anthropology and the author of the bestselling book *Changing Traditions in the Modern World*. First of all, could you tell us what anthropologists study and what is your own area of interest?

Robert: That's a good question! Anthropology, in a general sense, is the study of humanity. I know that's not very exact. That's why we have many types of anthropology, like linguistic anthropology, or social anthropology. My specialisation is cultural anthropology. I study different cultures around the world and how social and political changes affect these cultures.

Presenter: And when did you first become interested in anthropology?

Robert: I grew up in a multicultural house. My mother is British and my father is Korean. They were both English teachers, so we travelled a great deal. As a child, I lived in Japan, Thailand and Egypt. That's why I decided to study Anthropology. Growing up in different cultures helps you realise that customs and traditions are often local. Things that are acceptable in one culture can be completely unacceptable in another. However, despite some differences between cultures, I have noticed that there are often more similarities than differences between people.

Presenter: And do traditions change?

Robert: Absolutely, customs and traditions change all the time. Some traditions die out because our way of life changes, but most traditions adapt.

Presenter: As I understand it, that's one of the main points of your latest book.

Robert: Yes. My book is about the effect of modern technology on traditions around the world. It's well known that things such as electricity, the telephone, and television have changed our lives significantly. The introduction of these inventions into our lives has changed many of our customs. For example, in the past, families spent time playing board games, or listening to the radio in the evening. These activities would deepen family relationships. Now, due to developments in technology, people spend more time interacting with other people over the internet.

Presenter: Is that a bad thing?

Robert: I don't think so. There are people who complain about the changes that technology has brought to our lives. Personally, I think these changes are fine. We still spend time interacting with other people, but it's not always face-to-face.

Presenter: In your book, you discuss how technology has changed the way we celebrate important holidays.

Robert: That's right. A simple example is sending cards or messages. In the past, people sent each other cards to celebrate important events like birthdays or anniversaries. But now, more people send messages through social-networking sites or by email. Another example of changing customs is holiday food. A few generations ago, people spent a lot of time and effort preparing special meals for celebrations. It was usually the women who did this. Some dishes could take up to a week to prepare. But now we don't have to work so hard. The reason for this is we have modern kitchens and supermarket food. We don't have to spend endless hours making our own butter or bread any more. Everything is quicker and easier now.

Presenter: I remember my grandmother working for days to make food. She had a huge recipe book that she got from her grandmother. Everything had to be exactly as it was when she was a little girl.

Robert: That's a good example of a tradition that has been replaced by technology. You can find any recipe you want on the internet. This means that many people don't need recipe books anymore. Another thing is that many families now go out instead of cooking at home. In India, for example, families hire catering companies to provide food for weddings or special occasions. In the US during Thanksgiving, which is one of the biggest celebrations there, many families go to restaurants, because they don't want to spend their holidays working in the kitchen.

Presenter: So, people do continue their tradition of eating a special meal – they just do it in a different way.

Robert: Yes. Traditions don't always die out – but customs and traditions do change and adapt to the modern world.

 2.6

Yildiz: So our assignment is about customs and traditions in the modern world. What do you think about social-networking sites?

David: Pardon? I'm not sure I understand. What do you mean by customs on social-networking sites?

Yildiz: What I mean is the new rules that people have started to follow when they use social-networking sites. After all, customs are rules of behaviour, aren't they?

🔊 **2.7**

Dora: OK. I think I know what you mean. For example, you can write a 'happy birthday' message online for everyone to see. Sorry, but that's really lazy. Whenever any of my friends have a birthday, the website tells me about it. I don't need to make an effort. All I have to do is click and send a quick 'happy birthday' message. Where's the personal touch? But, if I don't send one, my friend will get upset.

Yildiz: I couldn't agree more. Last week one of my friends had her birthday, so I said 'happy birthday' when I met her, in real life. She said she was sad because I hadn't written anything on her profile page.

David: Yes, social networking has changed how we behave with our friends. Another new custom is that I feel I have to click the *like* button whenever my friends upload a photo.

Dora: What do you mean?

David: You know, there's a *like* button under each photo. So whenever my friends upload something, they expect me to *like* it. If I don't, they ask me the next day if I've seen their photo. And most of the photos that people upload aren't so interesting. It seems pointless to me.

Dora: I totally agree. I get tired of it. It seems that's another new custom – taking photos wherever you go and putting them on the internet. Last year, I went to a concert with a friend. He hardly saw anything of the concert because he was too busy taking photos of himself and putting them online. I was thinking to myself, 'Why don't you just enjoy the concert?' It's really annoying.

Yildiz: No, I completely disagree. I think that it's nice that people post news about exciting or interesting things that happen to them. I like to see what other people are doing. It's just sharing information.

David: I'm not convinced. Is it sharing or is it showing off? I think people upload pictures of themselves on holidays or at concerts just because they want to show others how amazing their lives are.

Yildiz: OK, but what about when you get married or have a new baby? Why not share it online with other people? Personally, I don't have a problem with it.

David: Sorry, I don't agree. I think that personal events should be for family or close friends. Your real friends will know about the event anyway, so why tell the whole world about it?

Dora: Actually, I have to disagree. Since I've been in the UK, I've missed my family, and so I upload photos almost every day, so they can see what I'm doing and where I live. It's an easy, cheap way to stay in touch with people back home.

David: OK, yes. That's a good point. There are situations when sharing photos is not about showing off. OK, what ideas do we have so far?

Yildiz: I've been writing our ideas down, and we've discussed birthday messages, using the *like* button, and sharing photos. Can we think of anything else?

Dora: I think that's enough. Shall we do some more research, and then we can meet the professor to discuss the assignment?

UNIT 3

▶ The desert mummies of Peru

Presenter: In the dry Atacama desert in Peru, the sands reveal treasures more valuable than gold: the objects and remains of an ancient Peruvian people called the Chiribaya.

Hundreds of years ago, the dry air and sand of the desert naturally preserved and mummified the dead bodies of the Chiribaya people. For archeologists, these mummies are silent and powerful witnesses of ancient history.

The Chiribaya people lived in southern Peru, in a valley from the Pacific coast to around 40 kilometres inland.

At one time there were 30,000 people living in the valley, but not much is known about the culture of the Chiribaya people. Their simple buildings made of mud and sticks did not survive.

Everything archaeologists know about the Chiribaya comes from their tombs. They have discovered many treasures buried with the mummies, such as gold cups, earrings and

decorations. However, the archaeology has brought thieves looking for gold.

Interviewee: Greedy, greedy people. Just tomb after tomb. They would just get the mummy bundles or get the mummies and the word was that the gold was inside the mouth so they would separate the skull from the rest of the body and crack the skull. It's just awful and annoying that we can't stop it.

Presenter: Archaeologists must work fast to beat the thieves. A new tomb has been discovered. Inside the tomb is a complete mummy, wrapped in a striped blanket, with an offering of llama feet in a basket to represent food.

In a laboratory, the archaeologists unwrap the body. The head has grey hair. They then remove the body's blankets. This mummy was a very old man. The way his body was preserved shows he was an important member of Chiribaya society. It is the job of archaeologists to help reveal the secrets of the Chiribaya people. However, because of the destruction of the mummies by treasure hunters many mysteries of these ancient people will never be solved.

🔊 **3.1**

Ken: Did you have time to think about our History presentation?

Hakan: Not really. I had to study for a maths test. Can we do it now?

Ken: OK. We have to come up with a topic and then we can discuss who will prepare what.

Hakan: Sounds good to me. Has the professor sent us the list of possible topics to choose from?

Ken: Yes, it's here. So, the list includes some of the most important historical finds.

Hakan: Uhuh.

Ken: We have to choose one and give a ten-minute presentation about it.

Hakan: I see. Let's see what we have here. The Rosetta Stone looks interesting. From what I know it's very old. I think it's more than 2,000 years old.

Ken: And where is it from?

Hakan: It was created for the king of Egypt of that time, Ptolomy V. It contained information in three languages, in Greek, Demotic Egyptian and Egyptian hieroglyphs.

Ken: What's Demotic Egyptian?

Hakan: I'm not a hundred percent sure, but from what I understand, it's closer to the modern Egyptian language. When the Rosetta Stone was found in 1799, it helped researchers to understand the hieroglyphs.

Ken: OK. I see.

Hakan: Before that, the historians had no idea what the ancient Egyptian writing meant.

Ken: Do you mean that comparing Greek with Demotic Egyptian helped them read the ancient Egyptian writing?

Hakan: That's how I understand it. And so, thanks to the Rosetta Stone, historians learned about ancient Egyptian beliefs and culture.

Ken: That sounds interesting. But let's see what else we can talk about. I don't think I can explain the Rosetta Stone clearly to the other students.

Hakan: No, it's not easy.

Ken: What about the Terracotta Army. I saw a documentary about it on TV.

Hakan: I've heard about it, but I don't know much about it. What is the Terracotta Army?

Ken: Well, terracotta is a type of ceramic. It was an army of statues – discovered in the 1940s by a Chinese farmer. These warriors were buried underground next to the tomb of the Chinese Emperor Qin Shi Huang. He believed the soldiers would protect him in the afterlife. I think they found 10,000 of them. Some of them are human and some are animals.

Hakan: Do you know how old it is?

Ken: Again, it's more than 2,000 years old.

Hasan: Like the Rosetta Stone, then. And what did the historians learn from it?

Ken: The interesting thing is that the warriors had real weapons. Historians analysed the army. They discovered how the Chinese army was organized and what weapons they used.

Hakan: Interesting.

Ken: I think so, but it might be too difficult to explain all the weapons they used. What do you think?

Hakan: Yes, you're right. We need to choose something that won't be too difficult to explain.

Ken: Yes, I know what you mean. What about Tutankhamun's Tomb?

Hakan: That's a good idea. It's interesting and easy to explain.

Ken: Yes, exactly.

Hakan: What information do we have about it?

Ken: In the book it says that the tomb, which is located in the Valley of the Kings in Egypt, was discovered in 1922.

Hakan: And do we know anything about Tutankhamun?

Ken: Yes, there's plenty of information about him. He was an Egyptian king and he died at a very young age. Historians think that the tomb was built for somebody else but because the ruler died when

he was so young, they had to use it. It says here that it took eight years to find everything that was inside. But from this, we learned a lot about life in ancient Egypt and their religious beliefs.

Hakan: Do you know what was inside the tomb?

Ken: There were hundreds of objects, like statues, jewellery, lamps … It contained everything that a king would need in his afterlife. Although, I'm not sure how old the tomb is?

Hakan: Well, it's the oldest of our topics. I think it's about 3,500 years old.

Ken: OK. Well, let's try and do the presentation on Tutankhamun. So what part do you want me do work on … ?

🔊 **3.6**

Good Morning! Let's begin. Last week, we discussed how the Ottoman Empire was founded. As you may remember, we discussed that the Ottoman Empire lasted for 623 years, in the period from 1299 until 1922. In the 16th century, it was one of the most powerful states in the world. If you look at the map, you will notice that the eastern borders of the empire covered the region of south-eastern Europe – that is, modern day Greece and Bulgaria. In the south, it included Egypt, Algeria and Yemen, and in the east, Azerbaijan, Armenia and Iraq. Today, we will discuss one of the most important events in the history of the empire and the man who was behind it. The conquest of Constantinople by Mehmed II was one of the turning points in the history of the empire. First, we will look at the political situation in Constantinople in the 15th century. Then, we will discuss the conquest of the city, and finally the role played by Mehmed II in its development. Constantinople, which in modern times is known as Istanbul, was founded by the Roman emperor, Constantine the Great, in 330 AD. By the 15th century, the city was the capital of the Byzantine Empire. 'Byzantine' is the term used for the Roman Empire in the Middle Ages. In the 1100s, Constantinople was the richest place in Europe. In the 1400s, the city had approximately 70,000 inhabitants. Constantinople was famous for its defence system. It was protected by a double wall. In addition to this, the Golden Horn and the Sea of Marmara provided protection. Despite the excellent defences, the city was captured in 1453 by Mehmed II, a sultan of the Ottoman Empire, and shortly after, it became the capital of the Ottoman Empire.

🔊 **3.7**

So who was Mehmed? Mehmed II, or as he is sometimes referred to, 'Mehmed the Conqueror', is probably one of the greatest military rulers in the history of the world. He was born in 1432 and at the age of 21, he led an army of 200,000 men and 320 ships to take over Constantinople. It took him just 53 days to conquer the city. Mehmed was an excellent planner and he hired engineers to build modern weapons. As soon as he took over Constantinople, Mehmed started re-building the city and encouraged people to move there. Meanwhile, he also made it the capital of the Ottoman Empire and founded many universities and colleges. The sultan invited educated men from all over Europe to come and live in Constantinople. Mehmed himself is said to have been fluent in seven languages, including Turkish, Arabic, Persian, Hebrew, Greek and Latin, and perhaps Russian. Eventually, Mehmed II ruled the Ottoman Empire from 1451 until his death in 1481. During this period, he became famous for his conquests all over Europe and Asia. In addition to Mehmed's military conquests and language skills, he was the first to write laws for the Ottoman Empire. His rule expanded the Ottoman Empire across Europe and in Asia. Constantinople, or as we know it today, Istanbul, was the capital of the Ottoman Empire for 469 years, from 1453 until 1922. Much of the city's unique atmosphere and beauty is due to Mehmed II and his vision. Next week, we will discuss the role of the Ottoman Empire in the 16th and 17th centuries. Your assignment for this week is …

🔊 3.9

| travelled | crossed | visited | lasted | returned |
| missed | described | died | helped | |

UNIT 4

▶ How to make a BMW

How can you make an environmentally friendly car that still drives at fast speeds? Cars that run on diesel fuel rather than petrol are often considered dirty and old-fashioned. However, German car-maker BMW has developed the technology to make diesel engines cleaner, bringing them into the 21st century. Old diesel engines were made of iron and were very heavy, but the new BMW engine cases are made of aluminium and are 40% lighter. This makes their cars much more efficient, as they can travel further on less fuel. The BMW factory in Austria makes 700,000 engines a year, but the engines are fitted inside the cars 5 hours away in Germany.

The BMW factory in Germany is one of the most modern in the world. Almost every process is automated. The cars are assembled with huge robots.

This is the exhaust unit.

The engine and exhaust are added to the chassis and suspension. Robot carts take them to the final part of the factory line. At this stage, the engine is combined with the body of the car. This only takes 80 seconds. The BMW factory can produce 44 cars an hour.

The last part of the process is attaching the badge to the finished car.

BMW cars can reach speeds of up to 270 kilometres per hour. Through a combination of modern technology and high power, the company ensures that their cars are some of the fastest and cleanest on the road.

🔊 4.3

Presenter: Have you ever been afraid of flying? Do you feel scared when you sit on a plane? Are you stressed when there's turbulence? If so, you may have aerophobia. The word *aerophobia* comes from the Greek, and it consists of two parts: *aero* which means 'flight' or 'air', and *phobia* which means 'fear'. People with aerophobia experience extreme fear or panic when they sit on a plane. In today's programme, we are going to discuss some steps that you can take to reduce this fear. With me today is Mark Knowling. Mark used to be a flight attendant who was afraid of flying. He has written a book about his experience and often gives presentations to help other people deal with their phobias. Can you tell us more about your experience, Mark?

Mark: Yes, sure. So I joined a flight attendant's course right after college. My goal was to see the world and I thought it would be a good job for me. On the course, I learnt a lot more than I expected. During the training, we studied a lot about air safety but there were also lectures about plane crashes. The instructors would tell us horrible stories of broken engines, birds hitting the aircraft, and hijackings, and even stories of planes crashing in the middle of the desert or in the ocean.

Presenter: That's terrible!

Mark: No, I don't think so. I believe they were trying to make us take the job seriously. They would also discuss the research done by air-crash investigators to help us understand the reasons behind air crashes. There is a detailed record of each crash, which investigators check carefully.

Presenter: But for you, I suppose this training had the opposite effect. Did it make you afraid of flying?

Mark: Uhuh, I actually became very scared of being on a plane. When I told my colleagues about it, they just laughed. They couldn't believe that I had completed the flight attendant training and now I was afraid to get on a plane. What was I supposed to do? I decided to do some research online and I read stories of people who managed to control their fear of flying.

Presenter: Can it be cured?

Mark: Actually, like any phobia, you can't always cure it, but you can decrease its effects on your life. You need to have the right attitude. You can achieve anything if you concentrate and stay positive. The advice I got was very useful, but it was a challenge, and it took me a long time to get over my fear.

🔊 **4.4**

Presenter: Can you share some advice with our listeners?

Mark: Of course. Well, the first method is to learn more about how planes work. For example, many people believe that without the engines, the plane will simply fall down from the sky. This is not true. The plane will stay up because its wings push against the air. A plane can fly without the engines and a well-trained pilot will be able to control it without power. All pilots learn how to fly without the engines.

Presenter: What about turbulence? Whenever I fly, I get very scared during turbulence.

Mark: Well, turbulence can be dangerous, yes of course. However, most turbulence is completely normal, and will not cause any problems, so you shouldn't be afraid of it. The only situation when it can cause problems is when the aircraft is already damaged or during a storm. But, as you know, most airlines study the weather and will not transport passengers if they think the weather conditions are not suitable for flying.

Presenter: Is there any other advice that you can give?

Mark: Understanding where the emergency exits are may help you relax. Not knowing where an exit is and feeling that you are in a closed space can make you afraid. Finally, to decrease the fear of flying, you should avoid watching films about plane crashes or other accidents. Some researchers say that aerophobia is caused by people watching too many disaster movies. I think we often forget that, compared to the many forms of transport that we use every day, air transport is actually very very safe.

Presenter: In what way?

Mark: Well, there is research which compares the number of accidents per number of kilometres travelled in each form of transport. We can see that by far the safest form of travel is air transport

and the most dangerous is using a motorbike. In recent years, there has been a significant decrease in the number of plane crashes. In contrast, cars are considerably more dangerous.

Presenter: Really? I didn't know that. Thank you for your advice Mark. You can let us know what you think about air safety and share your stories by going to our website at …

🔊 **4.6**

Peter: Hello, thank you all for coming here today to help us with our research. As you may have read in the email, my colleagues and I are working on our post-graduate research. Our topic is cycling in big cities and we're really interested in hearing about your experience of cycling in London. Thanks for responding to our email request. So, you're all cyclists?

Eva: Yes, I'm Eva, I'm a student here and I cycle every day from the hall of residence to my lectures.

Anna: I'm Anna and I work in the HR department, but I also cycle to work every day. Well, when it's not raining.

Liam: Hello, I'm Liam. Actually, I don't cycle regularly, only at the weekend and when the weather is nice, but I hope I can help with your research.

Peter: That's fine. OK, so as you may know, more and more people have started cycling in recent years. Can you tell me why you cycle?

Eva: For me, it's the convenience. The university residence is only 7 km away from the campus. In the past, I used to take the bus, but I hated it. I had to wait ages for it to arrive. It was always late. And inside the bus, it's so crowded you can't move. Last year, someone stole my mobile from my bag. That's when I decided to get a bicycle. For me, a bicycle is much more comfortable than public transport. I just jump on my bike anytime and go wherever I want. Plus, it's free.

Liam: As I said, I don't cycle every day. I go out at the weekend with my family, so for me it's just for fun. It's something to do at the weekend. I wouldn't cycle to work. I think the traffic in the city is crazy and there is very little space left for cyclists. I've seen cars driving in the bicycle lanes to overtake other cars. Riding a bike is definitely more difficult in a big city. It's not for me. What about you, Anna?

Anna: I see your point, but I've been cycling for over eight years now and I love it. First, I started cycling to work to lose weight. I work long hours and I don't have much time for exercise, so I thought it would be a great idea to get some on the way to work. In my opinion, cycling is the fastest and the greenest way to travel in the city. But I agree that it can be dangerous, and many car drivers have no respect for cyclists. They think they own the road. A lot of cyclists put cameras on their helmets in case they get hit by a car.

🔊 **4.7**

Peter: So what do you think can be done to improve the experience of cyclists?

Anna: Well, first of all, I think it would be safer if they made more bike lanes in the city. Also, the lanes should be wider, to allow more bicycles to pass at the same time.

Eva: I agree. Also, I'd like it if they somehow separated the lanes from the main road to protect cyclists. If there's an accident involving a car and a bicycle, the cyclist is always terribly injured. They ought to do something to prevent this happening.

Liam: Well, yes, but does the government have the money to make more bike lanes? I think it would be much better if the police gave heavy fines to drivers who break the law. So, for example, if a policeman sees a car in a bike lane, they should issue a heavy fine. This will prevent cars hitting cyclists and will even save lives.

🔊 **4.8**

A: I'm really surprised by these statistics. I didn't know that eating while driving is dangerous. I don't think the government should do anything about it. Personally, I eat fast food in my car a few times a week and I've never had an accident. And I'm not convinced that driving while eating is a big problem. Have you ever eaten while driving?

B: No, I haven't. We should take this really seriously. I think it would be better if they closed drive-through restaurants. This is because they only encourage drivers to buy food and eat it while they drive. How can you focus on the road if you're holding a big hamburger in your hand? It seems dangerous to me. What do you think?

C: I completely agree. I think it would be much better if drivers weren't allowed to eat or drink while they drive. From my own experience, I can tell you that it can be very dangerous. Last week, I bought some coffee and something to eat on the way to work. As I was driving, I had to brake suddenly and I spilled hot coffee over my legs. I almost lost control of the car. I think the police should give heavy fines if they see someone doing it.

D: OK, I understand, but it might be very difficult for the police to see drivers eating, especially if they are driving fast. The best thing would be to have more cameras on the roads to record what drivers are doing. The reason for this is the police can check the videos to see who is eating, who is texting, and so on. Then, I suggest that the police give the drivers points on their licence. If the driver has a lot of points, the police should take his or her car away for a week.

🔊 **4.9**

A well-known internet clip shows a young man falling into a fountain in a shopping mall. It happened when the man was busy sending a text on his mobile phone while walking. The video has started a debate about whether the government should ban texting and walking. The city of Fort Lee in New Jersey has starting giving fines of over $50. The authorities hope that people will pay more attention while crossing the road, and that the streets will become safer.

UNIT 5

▶ Sleeping giants: Russia's giant volcanoes

Presenter: In the east of Russia, nine hours from Moscow, lies one of the most active volcanic regions on earth: Kamchatka.

The Kamchatka region is as big as California, but only 400,000 people live there, surrounded by 300 volcanic sites. Vulcanologist Sasha Ovsyannikov has worked in the volcanoes of Kamchatka for 35 years. Among the most active volcanoes in the region is Mutnovsky. It was formed 45,000 years ago when four smaller volcanoes collapsed, into one vast volcano cone. It is 1.5 km across.

Sasha is checking the activity in the volcano. It could explode at any moment, releasing dangerous clouds of ash and gas into the air. But Sasha feels no fear.

Sasha: You cannot help but fall in love with volcanoes because they are like living things. They live their own lives and each erupts in its own way. Like people, volcanoes are all different.

Presenter: He takes samples of rock and gas from the volcano to see whether Mutnovsky is about to erupt. Sasha works with scientists at a volcano institute. They check Sasha's rock samples and monitor the 19 big volcanoes in the region and try to predict the next eruption. The volcanoes of Kamchatka are a threat to the aircraft that cross the region. Ash from an eruption can rise 14 km above the ground and travel thousands of km. The rock and dust in the ash can damage a plane's engine and cause it to crash.

Sasha and his colleague fly to another volcano 100 kilometres away, called Karymsky, to investigate how active it is. When they arrive, everything seems calm, but suddenly, without warning, Karymsky erupts. An explosion of this size is very unusual.

A week later, Sasha and his pilot decide it is safe enough to fly over the crater of Karymsky.

Thanks to the work of Sasha and other scientists, the world's airlines will be warned immediately if Karymsky, or any other volcanoes in Kamchatka, are likely to explode again soon.

🔊 **5.2**

Good morning. As you may remember, the last lecture focused on issues of climate change, its causes and effects. Today, I want to explain some alternative solutions that may help reduce some of the problems related to climate change. The first solution uses solar energy to grow food in the desert. That's right, growing fruit and vegetables in the desert is now possible and the first desert farms have been built in Australia. First of all, I will explain how farming in the desert works. Then, we will briefly discuss how this type of farming could solve some of the environmental problems we are now facing. And finally, we will discuss some possible problems of this system. So how does it work? As we all know, in order to grow plants we need water and sunlight. While we have a lot of sunlight in the desert, we have very little water. Scientists have decided to combine the modern technology of solar energy with a farming technology called 'hydroponics'. Hydroponics means growing plants in water. In the 1700s, scientists observed that plants don't need to grow in the ground. What we need are nutrients, or chemicals that help plants grow. Nutrients are like food for the plants. Therefore, if you add the nutrients to water, you can grow your fruit and vegetables in water. NASA scientists have been developing this method of growing food, because it could allow us to grow food in any climate – in Antarctica, the Sahara desert, or even on Mars. You might ask how this method of growing plants helps with the problem of global warming. I mean, after all, it uses fresh water, which is a limited resource on our planet.

An Australian company, Sundrop Farms System, combined hydroponics with solar energy. Traditional farming uses between 60–80% of our planet's fresh water. However, Sundrop Farms doesn't use fresh water. They use sea water. Sundrop Farms are only 100 metres from the sea shore. A line of mirrors reflects heat from the sun onto a pipe, a pipe which has oil inside. The hot oil in the pipe heats up sea water, which is inside

special containers. When the sea water reaches 160°C, the steam from this process provides electricity. Some of the hot water is used to heat the greenhouse during the cold desert nights. The rest of the heated water goes to a desalination plant. 'Desalination' means removing the salt from sea water to create clean, drinkable water. The desalination plant can produce up to 10,000 litres of fresh water every day. The farmer adds nutrients to the water and then grows fruit and vegetables.

To summarise, the solar energy is used to remove the salt from the sea water, and the fresh water is then used inside the greenhouse, where the plants are growing. As you can imagine, many people around the world are really excited about this technology. So far, Australian farms have grown tomatoes, peppers and cucumbers in this way. Many supermarkets are interested in buying these vegetables because they are grown without chemicals. Some people think this is the perfect solution to the world food crisis. After all, this way of farming can help us grow food in very difficult conditions. Furthermore, it uses sea water, which is a major advantage.

Finally, the desert farms use solar energy and not fossil fuels, thus their negative effect on the environment is minimal. Taking all this into consideration, the quality of food, the use of sea water and the minimal use of fossil fuels, I think that desert farms might be a very interesting way to farm in the future. Now let's discuss some of the problems ...

🔊 **5.3**

An Australian company, Sundrop Farms System, combined hydroponics with solar energy. Traditional farming uses between 60–80% of our planet's fresh water. However, Sundrop Farms doesn't use fresh water. They use sea water. Sundrop Farms are only 100 metres from the sea shore. A line of mirrors reflects heat from the sun onto a pipe, a pipe which has oil inside. The hot oil in the pipe heats up sea water, which is inside special containers. When the sea water reaches 160°C, the steam from this process provides electricity. Some of the hot water is used to heat the greenhouse during the cold desert nights. The rest of the heated water goes to a desalination plant. 'Desalination' is when we remove the salt from sea water to create clean, drinkable water. The desalination plant can produce up to 10,000 litres of fresh water every day. The farmer adds nutrients to the water and then grows fruit and vegetables.

To summarise, the solar energy is used to remove the salt from the sea water, and the fresh water is then used inside the greenhouse, where the plants are growing. As you can imagine, many people around the world are really excited about this technology. So far, Australian farms have grown tomatoes, peppers and cucumbers in this way. Many supermarkets are interested in buying these vegetables because they are grown without pesticides or other chemicals. Some people think this is the perfect solution to the world food crisis. After all, this way of farming can help us grow food in very difficult conditions. Furthermore, it uses sea water, which is a major advantage.

Finally, the desert farms use solar energy and not fossil fuels, thus their negative effect on the environment is minimal. Therefore, the quality of food, the use of sea water, and the minimal use of fossil fuels, I think that desert farms might be a very interesting way to farm in the future. Now let's discuss some of the problems …

🔊 5.5

A: Welcome to today's debate on the advantages and disadvantages of nuclear energy. Some people think that nuclear power is an environmentally friendly source of energy because there is less pollution than traditional power plants. However, the opponents of nuclear energy believe that there are more dangers than benefits.

B: That's right. I want to argue that there are many problems with nuclear power. It may be true that there are very few accidents caused by nuclear plants, but if there is an accident, then it will be huge, and have long-term effects on the environment. For example, after the Fukushima nuclear disaster in Japan, the government had to tell people to leave their homes because of the possibility of radiation. The radioactive material spread to water and food, such as tea, milk, beef and fish. For months after the accident, the Fukushima plant was dangerous. People will not be able to live in the nearby area for the next 20 years. This is the big risk of building a nuclear power plant.

C: I have to disagree. I think we should look at the bigger picture. Some people are worried that nuclear power is a big risk. Despite that, there are hundreds of nuclear power plants all over the world and there have only been three nuclear accidents in the last 30 years. In fact, research shows that many more people die while working with coal, natural gas, and hydropower. Furthermore, nuclear power is the most environmentally friendly and the most sustainable source of energy. A nuclear power plant does not pollute the air, it is relatively cheap, and it can provide a huge amount of electricity to our cities. And of course, our cities are growing.

B: I'm sorry, can I interrupt? Some people say that nuclear energy does not pollute the air, but that's not completely true. It takes many years to build a nuclear power plant. During this time, hundreds of machines work day and night and pollute the air in the area. I don't think it's necessary to build nuclear power plants, when we have safer and more environmentally friendly energy sources, such as solar or wind energy. They are cheaper and they are unlimited sources of energy. Furthermore, they are more affordable for most countries, when compared with nuclear power. Building a nuclear power plant is not a solution for poor or developing countries.

C: I'm not sure about that. I think that building nuclear power plants is the perfect solution for many poorer countries. Yes, it might be expensive to build the plant, but once the nuclear plant is there, the cost of the production of energy is very low. What's more, the country can sell the electricity to its neighbours and improve its economy. It's a long-term solution. Moreover, it makes a country less dependent on oil and gas. At the moment, whenever oil or gas prices go up, it's the poor countries and poor people who suffer. Some people think that solar or wind energy are greener than nuclear energy. However, I don't think that's accurate. Wind turbines are not friendly for birds. Not to mention that solar panels and wind turbines take up a lot of space. They are also very expensive and do not last as long as a nuclear power plant.

A: Thank you both very much. Let's take some questions from the audience …

UNIT 6

▶ Training for a triathlon: the ultimate event

Rian Gonzales is a 39-year-old computer programmer from California. He is overweight. To help lose weight he has run six marathons. His goal is now to participate in the Malibu triathlon. A triathlon is a fitness event where participants swim, cycle and run. The Malibu triathlon consists of an 800 metre swim, a 30 kilometre bike ride and a 6 and a half kilometre mile run. The hardest part of the triathlon for Rian will be the swim. He is afraid of the water because he almost drowned as a child. He hires a swimming coach to help him train. Soon he can swim twice as far as he was able to a week ago. To help in the cycling section of the triathlon, Rian goes to a specialist shop and gets some professional cycling clothes and shoes to wear. Rian is given a bike to ride made of carbon fibre and aluminium, which is very light. He goes out cycling and soon feels a lot more comfortable on the bicycle. A week before the triathlon, Rian collects his wet suit. This will keep him warm when he does the triathlon sea swim. He puts on the wetsuit and goes training with a friend. He swims 400 metres in the ocean, half the distance he needs to swim in the competition. He is almost ready to take part in the triathlon.

The day of the triathlon arrives. Rian is nervous but he gets ready to enter the water. The triathlon starts and he begins the swim.

He gets out of the water and starts the cycling part of the race. The bike ride is tough.

Rian runs the third part of the triathlon. Finally he finishes the race. His friends meet him at the end. Rian has now accomplished the goal of finishing his first triathlon, and hopes to do many more in the future.

🔊 6.1

Today we are talking about the key to a long and happy life. Recent studies of people who live to be 100 years old have shown that a healthy diet and exercise may not be enough. In fact, many of the people who celebrate their 100th birthday have smoked at some time in their lives, and never exercised regularly. This has led many people to believe that our lifestyles are not important. What's most important is that we have good genes. It seems that if you have the right genes, then you will live for a long time, whatever you do.

🔊 6.2

Presenter: So, new research shows that having a healthy lifestyle is not the most important thing, if you want a long life. We asked four people in the street for their views.

Speaker A: I think it's great news! Most people think that if they eat healthily and exercise, they will live forever. These people never drink coffee or sugary drinks. They spend hours working out in the gym or doing yoga. And none of this matters if you have the wrong genes. I think the key to a healthy life is to enjoy yourself. If you focus all your energy on what to do and what not to do, you'll be unhappy eventually. There is no question that happy people live longer. I'd much rather go out and have a pizza with friends than spend time in the gym.

Speaker B: This research proves what I've known for a long time. It's ridiculous to get too worried about healthy eating and exercise! My grandfather lived until he was 95, even though he never exercised. He ate lots of sugar and never had salads. He was brought up in a different world. He had different habits. He certainly never went to a gym. Yes, I'm sure that genes are more important than our lifestyle. Of course, I'm not going to take up smoking or eat fast food every day. It means I should keep fit, because it makes me feel better – but I won't allow it to take over my whole life.

Speaker C: Well, first of all, I prefer to exercise and eat well. What's wrong with being healthy? I also think that you won't know whether you have the right genes or not until you get ill. So why take the risk and be unhealthy? Also, don't forget that you might get the flu or a cold much more easily when you don't eat proper food or exercise. I'd say that it's always better to have a healthy lifestyle. Also, there is no doubt that bad health habits increase the chances of getting a serious illness.

Speaker D: Oh, that's great. So now we should all eat fast food and stop exercising? I mean … I look around and I see overweight children. No matter how good your genes are, these children will not be able to enjoy a long and healthy life unless they give up chips, chocolate bars, sugary drinks … Well, it's great that some people can live to be 100 and do whatever they want in their lives, but most of us don't have great genes and we have to be careful to take care of ourselves.

🔊 6.5

1 Do you feel tired and stressed? Do you have problems concentrating on your work? Do you want to discover your true self? If so, it's time to take up meditation. As we all know, meditation can improve your health and concentration. This ancient practice is known to increase your energy and lead to a happier life. Whether you are looking for a stress-free life, physical well-being or self discovery, Sanjee Meditation has it all. Sign up now for a free introduction class, starting on 15 January.

2 Aloe vera is the natural choice for your whole family. Our aloe vera products will make you look and feel better. Extracts from this plant have been used in beauty products for thousands of years. Our simple, but effective creams and shampoos will improve your skin and hair. Aloe vera juice is a healthy option for people with stomach problems. Our products help you improve your health naturally. Visit our website for more information about the benefits of our products.

3 Imagine a world of scents: the warm scent of sandalwood during your yoga classes; the scent of fresh jasmine as you relax at the seaside. Lime, lavender, frankincense – these scents have been our best friends for centuries. They can help you relax and they can reduce pain. Our health centre offers aromatherapy to help with your skin and sleep problems. Our oils come from organic gardens and contain only natural ingredients. Call us now for an appointment. Let the world of scents take you away!

4 Are you interested in alternative treatments? Have you ever wanted to explore the secrets of traditional Chinese medicine? This spring, join our six-month course in acupuncture. The course covers the theory of acupuncture and practical skills in using needles. Acupuncture is known to reduce pain, but it's also a great alternative for people who want to lose weight in an easy way. Learn more about the course and visit us on our open days on the first Saturday of every month.

UNIT 7

▶ Engineering a ski resort in the desert

Dubai: famous for its business, modern architecture and great beaches, and shopping centres. The owners of a shopping centre had a dream: to build the best indoor ski resort in the world. Before then, the only way to ski was to ski on the sand: 'sand ski' or use snowboards and 'sand board'! Building an indoor ski resort was an ambitious plan in a country where the temperature is regularly over 30 degrees centigrade.

Ski Dubai has real snow and the world's longest indoor slope. It is built over a shopping centre.

The huge shopping centre is almost 600,000 square metres in size, and has two luxury hotels with 900 rooms, a 14-screen cinema, car parking for 7,000 cars and, of course, the ski resort.

To build Ski Dubai, engineers had to construct some of the ski slopes on the ground, and then moved them up to the top of the building.

They started by lifting a 90-metre section of slope 60 metres into the air and fixing it in place.

The section weighs the same as 20 jumbo jets. It took two days to lift and position it in the correct place. The lift started, but suddenly there was a problem. The computer system crashed and the slope was stuck in the air. However, an hour later the computer was fixed and the lift of the slope continued. Finally the job was completed and the engineers celebrated the achievement. However, on innovative projects like this there are always problems. The engineers found that there were problems with the cooling pipes. The welding work was bad and had to be replaced. The engineers also decided to replace all the rubber pipes under the ski slope. They should not have had metal connectors because if the cooling liquid leaked out, it could have melted the 6,000 tonnes of snow at Ski Dubai. This meant that they had to dig all the pipes out of the concrete, causing a major delay to the project. Meanwhile, a French company completed the chair lifts which take skiiers to the top of the slope. After three months of hard work, Ski Dubai was finally ready and the engineers filled it with snow. It may be 30 degrees outside, but the world's first ski resort in the desert opened successfully.

🔊 **7.1**

Welcome to the Museum of Science! The exhibition that we are about to see is called *Discovering Medieval Science*. As some of you may know, the Middle Ages have often been called the *Dark Ages*. During this tour, you will find out that they were not. The Middle Ages *were* an interesting time and they were full of scientific discoveries. Inventions and technology from India, Persia, China, North Africa and the Middle East were brought to Europe.

Many inventions and machines designed by medieval scholars are still in use today. And, some of these inventions are very common. For example, the first fountain pen was made in 953 for the caliph of Maghreb. Before then, people used bird's feathers and ink to write with. This method would often leave your fingers and your clothes covered with black ink. The caliph wanted a device that would not do this. So, the first fountain pen had a small container with ink inside and did not stain people's clothes or fingers while the user was writing. You can see a model of this fountain pen in Room 11B. In the same room, you will find medieval chess sets. The game of chess was first played in ancient India, but the modern version of the game was developed in Persia and brought to Spain in the 10th century. The English expression *checkmate*, used to end the game, comes from the Persian *Shah Mat* which means 'the king is helpless'. But, let's now move to some other inventions.

In rooms 12A and 12B we have works by the great medieval engineer, al-Jazari. Al-Jazari lived in 12th-century Turkey. His work *The Book of Knowledge of Ingenious Mechanical Devices* lists 100 different machines with instructions and diagrams explaining how to build them. In this exhibition, you can see models of some of the devices that were designed by al-Jazari. Here, you can see his mechanical clocks. These clocks work by the use of water and weights. However, his most important invention was the crank shaft. The crank shaft is a long arm that allows machines to move in a straight line. It was first used for watering gardens and farms. In more modern times, a crank shaft is used in motorcar engines.

As we move along, you will find one of the most important inventions of medieval times. This invention has changed the history of the world in ways that we can't even imagine. It's one of the Four Great Inventions of Chinese culture: gunpowder. Gunpowder was invented in the 9th century by Chinese scientists who wanted to find out how to live forever. It led to the invention of fireworks and weapons. The first instructions on how to make gunpowder were written in the 11th century by Zeng Gongliang, Ding Du and Yang Weide. Gunpowder has changed the way we fight wars and has truly affected the history of the world. Many people think gunpowder is *the* most important invention in history. Now, let's move to the next room, which is all about medieval medicine …

🔊 7.2

1 Inventions and technology from India, Persia, China, North Africa, and the Middle East were brought to Europe.

2 The game of chess was first played in ancient India, but the modern version of the game was developed in Persia and brought to Spain in the 10th century.

3 The crank shaft is a long arm that allows machines to move in a straight line.

4 As we move along, you will find one of the most important inventions of medieval times.

🔊 7.4

Good morning! In today's lecture I want to discuss an invention that has changed our lives. It has made a huge difference to the way we work, travel, communicate, and socialize with friends. Can you guess what it is? I'm talking here about mobile phone apps. The word *app* comes from *application*. Traditionally, applications were used in computers to help them perform better. However, with the invention of smartphones, the word *mobile app* or *app* is used to refer to phone applications. In this lecture, we will start by discussing the very first apps and their development. We will then discuss how apps have changed our lives. Finally, we will focus on some of the most popular apps used by people today.

7.5

I'd like to start by talking a little bit about the first apps. These were included with each smartphone. These types of apps were placed in the phones to help users access the internet, check emails, send texts, and so on. We can say that the first apps were designed to increase efficiency at work and help access important information. However, it was the second generation of apps that really changed things. These were downloadable apps. Users simply downloaded the app from the internet and installed them on their phones. Since their first introduction, the app market has grown beyond our expectations. The first app shop was opened in 2008. By 2011, it was reporting over 10 billion downloads. By 2012, an estimated 30 billion apps had been downloaded. These numbers have been growing ever since.

These numbers give us a good idea about how popular apps are and how quickly they have developed. They are, in fact, a worldwide phenomenon, as people from all over the world use apps for entertainment, travel, or communication. I'm going to briefly talk about how these apps changed our lives. First of all, many apps have allowed us to stay in touch with each other more effectively. If you are a business person, you can check your emails at any time, even during a meeting. Secondly, texting has become one of the leading forms of communicating. Many new apps allow us to do online banking using our smartphones, get GPS directions to places, and share photos on social media sites. They can recommend a new movie, a restaurant in your neighbourhood, or tell you about the weather. People use apps to organise their travel plans, share product reviews, or shop online. In fact, more people are beginning to use apps rather than internet browsers on their smartphones. Now, I'd like to mention another important area – gaming. Smartphone games are a huge business, and count for billions of downloads. Finally, the invention of apps has created a whole new IT sector. It is one of the fastest-growing industries, and the need for skilled software engineers is rising quickly.

OK, in the next part of the lecture, I will discuss some of the most common apps in more detail …

🔊 7.6

I would like to present an invention that has made the way we organize our work easier. It's a simple invention and most of you have used it in the past. It's a small yellow piece of paper which is known all over the world. It's the sticky note.

A sticky note, is a piece of paper with special glue on the back. Modern sticky notes can be any colour or shape. Sticky notes are simple to use. You can stick them on anything and the note will stay in place. The notes can be easily removed from any surface. First, I am going to talk about the history of this invention. Then, I will explain how it has made a difference to our lives.

UNIT 8

From function to fashion

Fashion is important to a lot of people, but many of the clothes that are fashionable today didn't start as fashion items. Some clothes start as something practical and become fashionable as more people start to wear them. For example, today, Missoni is a famous fashion house, known for its bold, bright patterns. But, Missoni didn't start by making fashionable clothes. Ottavio Missoni started Missoni fashion when he was young. He was an international athlete and made the tracksuits for the 1948 Olympics. After his sporting career was over, he opened a workshop making woollen tracksuits.

The Missoni family started making clothes with wool and now design other fashionable clothes. Tracksuits also became fashion items and are popular because of the comfortable fit and fun colours.

Other fashion clothes started as sports clothes too. In the 1970s, jogging became popular and people needed more running shoes. By the 1980s a lot of people owned running shoes and they wore them because they looked good and were comfortable. Celebrities started wearing them too. Running shoe companies started to design shoes just for fashion and not for running and they got famous sports stars to promote them.

Another fashion item we see every day is jeans. Jeans were invented by Levi Strauss. His first business sold tents and wagon covers to miners in California. The miners needed hard-wearing clothes and Strauss invented trousers for them made of canvas. Over the years he improved the design, adding rivets for strength, using a more comfortable denim material and dying the trousers dark blue to hide stains.

Up until the 1950s and 60s, jeans were worn by manual workers, like cowboys and steel workers, but they became really popular when movie stars such as Marlon Brando and James Dean started to wear them. People started wearing jeans, not just for doing hard work, but as everyday clothes. So, the fashionable clothes you wear every day might have started from less stylish beginnings.

 8.1

Clara: Have you got any ideas for our research project?

Adele: I've been looking, but to be honest, I've found nothing in the library. Can you give me a hand?

Clara: I've been reading about fashion in the future, new designs, interesting new technology, and all that.

Adele: Do you mean the kind of clothes that we will be wearing in the future?

Clara: Not really. It's more about future fabrics and how they are going to be used.

Adele: Well?

Clara: OK. I've found out that there are designers who create eco-clothes.

Adele: Eco-clothes?

Clara: These are clothes that are not only good for the community but they're also environmentally friendly. The designers make sure that the clothes are not made by people working in very poor or bad conditions. Local workshops are set up so that people can earn a good salary. And eco-friendly clothing can help protect the environment, too, apparently.

Adele: How does it work, exactly?

Clara: Well, there are fabrics that collect the energy from when you move. Then, the energy is converted into electricity.

Adele: Interesting. So, in the future, we could use this fabric to charge our mobile phones, our cameras, right?

Clara: Well, as long as you keep moving, yes!

Adele: It reminds me of smart fabrics. I saw an exhibition about them during the science festival. Some scientists are working on fabrics that can kill bacteria, or regulate body temperature.

Clara: Go on.

Adele: Well, these fabrics keep your body temperature the same whatever the weather. And I read that they can be used to make sports clothing, which would help people who exercise in very cold or very hot climates.

Clara: That's interesting.

Adele: I've also read that there are other fabrics that can help reduce muscle aches or prevent us from getting ill.

Clara: That's very interesting. I saw a fashion show once where the designers used lights in the clothes. It was a dress made from lights. They change colour as you move. It was very beautiful.

Adele: But what was the point of that?

Clara: Well, I do agree that it's not very practical. I don't think there are many people dying to wear a dress made of lights. It sounds like someone designed it just for the fun of it.

Adele: I'm not mad about that idea, to be honest. As far as I'm concerned, a dress made from lights is useless. Anyway, at long last, it looks like we've come up with some good ideas.

Clara: Yes, I agree. So, we have clothes that are environmentally friendly, clothes that help with our health, and clothes that use technology. Which one shall we focus on?

Adele: I like the idea of clothes that help people with health problems.

Clara: Are you sure? It seems complicated.

Adele: I do think it'll be interesting and there are a lot of different articles on this topic.

Clara: OK, let's do it!

 8.4

Presenter: In today's show, we'll be interviewing the talented fashion designer, Aysha Al-Husaini. Aysha's collection was presented during the most recent Fashion Week in Doha. She made a great impression on the audience with her unique designs which combine traditional Muslim fashion with French chic. Aysha – thank you for coming to the studio.

Aysha: Thank you for having me.

Presenter: First of all, can you tell me where you get your ideas from?

Aysha: Well, I come from a Muslim family. My parents are both from Qatar. I was born there but then we travelled a lot. I went to school in New York and I went to a design school there. These days, I spend my time travelling between Qatar and the US.

8.5

Presenter: How did you feel about growing up in New York?

Aysha: Well, as a teenager in New York, I had a lot of problems trying to dress in a modest way. For example, when you look at the summer fashion in New York, the trend is always to wear skirts, shorts and sleeveless shirts. I did not feel comfortable wearing them, but at the same time my friends thought it was strange to wear long sleeves and jeans in the summer. So I've always tried to combine my culture with fashion. As a teenager, I would make my own clothes, like colourful skirts and scarves. I wanted my designs to be individual. They were unique, and eventually, people admired my clothes, rather than laugh at me.

Presenter: Do you think that there is a lot of misunderstanding about Muslim clothes?

Aysha: I think so. The thing is that when you say *Muslim fashion*, people in New York think of a *burka*. You know, like the blue or black cloaks that cover women from head to toe.

Presenter: And what do you think Muslim fashion is?

Aysha: Let me give you an example – when I first started at design school, my teachers would ask me strange questions, such as how I was going to stay in the fashion business if I'm not going to design miniskirts or sleeveless shirts. But as far as I'm concerned, there is much more to fashion than showing your body. There are millions of Muslim women who live in the US and Europe who want to wear fashionable clothes. There are also women who simply like to dress in a modest way.

Presenter: So are you saying that there is a need for fashionable clothes for Muslim women?

Aysha: Absolutely. We want to be fashionable and be ourselves at the same time. My feeling is this – I want to create clothes that are modest but at the same time give women confidence – clothes that allow women to be themselves.

Presenter: I see what you mean. Many reviewers describe your style as 'traditional chic'. Would you agree with this?

Aysha: Yes, I would. What I think is that combining 'traditional' with 'chic' is a huge area in fashion. When you look at the work of other designers in China or India, you can see that many traditional styles are being re-used by young designers. Above all, people like to be individuals and show their cultural roots – they like to show where they come from.

Presenter: As I understand it, your designs are popular outside the US, is that right?

Aysha: Yes. As well as to New York and Paris, I sell my collection in big cities, like Doha, Dubai and Abu Dhabi. Another thing is that I also receive emails from women in Pakistan, Indonesia, Singapore and Malaysia about my clothes, and so perhaps in the future I might open shops there.

Presenter: Thank you for coming to the studio today.

Aysha: Any time!

UNIT 9

▶ Economic migration: the Chinese dream

During the last few decades, an economic revolution has taken place in China. In Chinese cities economic regulations have been relaxed and people are buying, selling and building to make money.

The result is the biggest economic migration in world history, as tens of millions of Chinese move from the countryside to urban areas in search of wealth and success.

Sun Feng came to Shanghai from his village a year ago. He is not alone: of a population of 20 million, over three million people in Shanghai are migrant workers. However, the only job he could find was one of the most dangerous in the city. He is a window cleaner, washing the city's skyscrapers. It is terrifying work. Sun Feng would like to buy a car, but the ones in this showroom are a fantasy for him. He must save the small amount of money he earns to feed his wife and baby daughter back in his home village.

High above the Shanghai streets at night, Sun Feng is still hard at work. Many Chinese companies want their windows cleaned at night so their workers are not disturbed during the day.

Sun Feng is unsure about the rich new world full of luxuries he has found in Shanghai. He believes that if China continues to develop economically, the country will lose some of its traditional, simple culture.

It is the Chinese New Year and Sun Feng is going back to his village to celebrate. When he left home his daughter was a baby and he hasn't seen her for a year. He misses her. It is one of the many sacrifices he has made by moving to Shanghai, following the economic dream of millions of Chinese people hoping for a better life.

🔊 9.1

In this week's programme, I would like to talk about a book that has changed the way I think about money. It's called *The secret of being wealthy*. It was written in 2005 by a business graduate called John Holm who decided to study the behavior of wealthy people. He paid close attention to what rich people do; checking where they eat, what they buy, how they live, and so on. The results of his study were rather surprising.

🔊 9.2

When you think of someone who is very rich, what comes to mind? Most people think that rich people drive very expensive cars, eat in expensive restaurants, own a yacht, or live in big houses. But, as John Holm discovered, people who have money don't actually do these things. Most millionaires actually seem to have ordinary lifestyles. They have normal cars, average houses, and so on. On the other hand, people who *look* rich – the people who drive the latest Ferrari, or only wear designer clothes – may not actually be rich at all. Instead, they have spent all their money trying to show off – showing other people that they might be wealthy.

So what do millionaires do, and what can we learn from them? The first, important thing is that millionaires always know how much they are spending. According to Holm, around 75% of millionaires know exactly how much money they have, and they know exactly how much they spend on food, bills, clothes, etc. This means that they don't spend too much, and they don't get into debt. They can plan for the future, and save their money. So, the lesson here is that you should never spend more money than you have!

Another surprising fact is that millionaires usually have simple lifestyles. They have nice houses and nice cars, but they don't spend all their money on these things. In fact, most rich people stay in the same place for a very long time, and don't live in big, expensive palaces. Indeed, according to John Holm, half of millionaires have lived in the same house for 20 years. Also, around 65% of millionaires live in homes which cost $350,000 or less. Again, the important lesson here is not to spend more money than you have. If you spend all your savings on a luxury BMW, then you probably aren't rich – you just want to look rich. In fact, the study reveals that 86% of luxury cars are bought by people who can't afford them. Most rich people do not have bank loans – they only spend a small percentage of what they have, and save or invest the rest.

Now here is an interesting fact. The study shows that most millionaires have very happy relationships. Not only are they married, but they stay married for a long time. In John Holm's opinion, this is very important because of the golden rule about saving money. There is no doubt that it's more difficult to save money if you are single. If there are two of you, it's easier to pay attention to what money you have, and what you are spending.

And of course, people who don't have huge bank loans and debts are happier. If you don't have to worry about the monthly credit-card payments, you are less likely to buy things to make you feel better. People with debts often spend more time shopping, just to improve their feeling of happiness, but real millionaires don't need to do this.

So what can we learn from the wealthy? The answer is surprisingly simple. Don't spend more money than you have. Don't get into debt or take out bank loans. Pay close attention to your money, and don't spend time trying to show other people that you are rich. In John Holm's opinion, being 'wealthy' is a feeling. It doesn't mean being rich or having millions of dollars. It means being happy with what you have.

🔊 9.4

In today's programme, we discuss the recent decision made by the Ministry of Education to give college students money in return for good grades. College students will be paid per hour to take additional Maths and Science classes. The students who improve their grades and keep their average score high will be given cash rewards in each semester. At the moment, this system is being tested in six colleges across the country. To discuss this new project, we have invited Dr Michael Burns from the Ministry of Education and we welcome your calls during the programme. Do you think college students should be paid for good grades?

🔊 9.5

Presenter: Dr Burns, thank you for coming today. Can you tell us more about the project? Where does this idea come from?

Dr Burns: Thank you. Well, the idea to pay college students for their work is not new. This programme has been used in the past in schools in the US. For example, in some schools in New York City, students are paid $50 for attendance and good grades, and in Baltimore, students who fail their exams are paid up to $110 to re-take their tests. The reason for these programmes is to encourage students to finish their education and be able to get a good job in the future. Many students who fail or drop out do so because they come from poor families. They might have to work after school and on the weekends to help support the family. Because of that, they often have no time to study. We want to make sure that all students have the same opportunities in their future.

Presenter: I see. Let's hear from our first caller. Mariam Hassan is a college director. Mariam?

Mariam: Hello. Yes, I recently read about this new programme and I disagree with it. I understand that many students drop out of college because

of financial problems. However, will paying students really encourage them to continue? Of course, the statistics are terrible. In my college alone, the dropout rate is over 25%, but I am not confident that this programme will solve the real problems or just cover them up. I think the money would be better spent on student services, like hiring additional teachers and advisors. Two of the reasons why students drop out are stress and poor time management.

Dr Burns: I can see your point, but we have already spent a lot on student services. I think that paying students to study will show them that we treat them like adults. It will give them a sense of responsibility. College students are young adults, and so when they have a choice between staying at college and studying or going to work and making money, they often make the wrong choice. They want to have money so that they can buy things for themselves. Besides, we don't want to pay them a lot. I think we are simply giving them an option: stay at school and be paid, or get a minimum-wage job.

Presenter: Christine Thorne is a parent with two children at college.

Christine: Hello. I was very worried when I heard about this new programme. I realize that students need encouragement to stay in school, but are we going in the right direction? First of all, I feel that we are sending the students the wrong message. Learning should be about studying new things and being responsible. Personally, I think the students who are not interested in studying will simply take the easy courses to keep their average score high and get the cash. I believe that we should focus more on rewarding excellent schools and teachers, and not on students who might be lazy.

Dr Burns: These are all good points, but I don't think that this view applies to all students. Not all parents are educated or interested in studying. They pass this bad attitude to their own children. Then, the children don't see the benefits of learning. To change this image, we need to show them a good reason for studying.

Presenter: Thank you. Let's have a look now at some of the emails we've received during the programme.

🔊 9.6

Aseel: I think that giving children money will teach them how to be responsible for their homework and housework. It will help them to understand the value of money, even if it's a very small amount. I give my child £10 every week for cleaning his room and studying spelling at home.

Joseph: Paying children for housework, like clearing or washing the dishes, is not a good idea. In my opinion, children should always work at home, because they are members of the family. They should be taught that it's their responsibility, and not a way to earn money. I think that paying children for housework is completely wrong.

Karen: I agree with the last speaker. Giving children money makes them ask for more all the time. They will think that they should receive money from their parents. I don't think it's OK to give children money for housework. They should learn to be helpful, and not expect a reward.

Robert: I disagree with some of the opinions I've heard here. I believe that giving children a small amount of money every week is an excellent way to teach them about the world of money. What's more, it's a very good way to teach them about maths.

🔊 9.7

Student 1: So why do you disagree with giving children money?

Student 2: It's because they start to think that it's their right to get money for nothing and they don't learn about hard work and how to earn money. They will think that money simply appears without any work.

Student 1: But what if they have to do something to get the money, like clean the family car or read a book? What do you think of that?

Student 2: I don't think that it's a good idea either. You shouldn't have to pay a family member to help you with something. For example, when my mother makes dinner, we don't pay her for it. She does it because she wants to. Paying children to do something in the house, or their homework, makes them think they should be paid for everything.

Student 1: But why shouldn't we encourage them to study?

Student 2: Because it won't encourage them. They will only do it for the money and that's wrong. We should teach them to study because it will benefit them in the future.

UNIT 10

▶ The placebo effect

Kate, a psychology student, is taking part in an experiment to test her brain's ability to respond to pain. She is going to be burned on her forearm without any painkillers. Her Professor, Tor Wager, places a metal plate the temperature of a very hot cup of coffee on her forearm. It is an uncomfortable experiment, designed to investigate the placebo effect.

The placebo effect occurs in the brain when a person is told that something will improve their health, or a painful condition, and they get better. However, nothing has actually been given or done to them to physically alter their condition.

Doctor Wager thinks that the power of suggestion actually produces a physical change in the brain, which is why placebo medicines can seem to have the same effects as real drugs. His plan is to look for changes in the part of the brain that senses pain while Kate is burned with the metal plate.

Kate enters a scanner. The professor burns her arm again and the scanner records her brain activity while she is in pain. Professor Wager then puts a cream on Kate's skin. He tells her that it is a powerful painkiller, but the lotion is a placebo. It is body cream, with nothing in it to stop the pain from the burns.

Kate enters the scanner again and she is burned at exactly the same temperature as before. This time, however, there is not as much activity in the pain centre of her brain. Kate actually feels a lot less pain, even though the lotion on her skin is not a painkiller.

The experiments show that the human brain's ability to recognise pain is flexible, as it can physically respond to a placebo by changing its signals. It seems the placebo effect really can work.

🔊 10.1

Presenter: What comes to mind when you hear the word *genius*? Most of us think of famous artists, musicians and scientists, like da Vinci, Beethoven or Einstein. These are people whose work has stood the test of time. The questions that many of us would like an answer to is: *What makes a genius?* Is being a genius determined by our genes or by our environment? In other words, are people born a genius or do they become a genius? To answer this question, I have invited here today psychologist Dr Erik Anderson, who has spent his career researching successful people.

🔊 10.2

Presenter: Dr Anderson, what does it mean to be a genius?

Dr Anderson: There's no precise definition of a genius. A genius is someone who is very special either in their intelligence or creativity. To put it another way, a genius can see ordinary things in a new light. That's why they can develop new theories, new trends in music and arts, and new inventions.

Presenter: In what ways are the brains of talented people different from ordinary brains?

Dr Anderson: That's a great question and I don't have a clear answer, but I can explain some theories that we have been developing over the years. Researchers study whether the brains of extremely intelligent people are different from average brains. Until now, there's been no definite evidence to support this theory.

Presenter: Some people say that extremely intelligent people are talented in many areas, like music and mathematics. Is that true?

Dr Anderson: It may be true, but it's a bit of a chicken and egg problem – what came first? Are the brains of extremely intelligent people naturally developed, or are they developed because they use them more? For example, Einstein used different areas of his brain. As a scientist, he used the logical part of his brain, but he also used the creative part when he came up with the theory of relativity, and when he played the violin in his free time. One thing that we know for sure is that geniuses are always busy doing things. This attitude helps develop your brain power.

Presenter: So, are you saying there's no such thing as a 'genius' brain?

Dr Anderson: I believe that genes may affect our brain function and our skills, but they don't determine them. However, there have been very special and talented people in the last 100 years, for example Bill Gates or Steve Jobs. Both men changed the way we communicate and work. Studies of their lives and work prove that genius is mostly hard work. It's the *10,000-Hour Rule*.

Presenter: What's the 10,000-Hour Rule?

Dr Anderson: It's a recipe for success. The theory states that if you put 10,000 hours into something, you will become an expert. That is, success is a direct result of a lot of hard work. According to Malcolm Gladwell, if you want to become successful at something you need to do it for 20 hours a week for 10 years.

Presenter: This theory reminds me of a famous saying by Edison.

Dr Anderson: 'Genius is 1% inspiration and 99% perspiration'? Is that what you mean?

Presenter: Yes, and he was a genius so he definitely knew what he was talking about!

Dr Anderson: I agree! What this saying means is that we need to be inspired or creative. But that's not enough. Real geniuses simply work hard.

Presenter: Thank you for the discussion. Let's hear from the audience.

🔊 **10.5**

Ella: Hello. Do you have a minute?

Claire: Yes. How can I help you?

Ella: I'm writing an article for the student newsletter about how to keep your brain active. And since you are the study counsellor, we thought we could ask you a few questions. Do you mind?

Claire: Not at all. So, what's your first question?

Ella: Well, first of all, we would like to know how important it is to keep your mind active.

Claire: As a student, it's extremely important, because your brain is your work tool. To start with, we have to understand that the brain is like a muscle. And so, how do you develop your muscles?

Ella: You exercise them?

Claire: That's right! You go to the gym, you go jogging or swimming, and so on. And what happens if you don't use your muscles? They become weak and waste away.

Ella: So what can we do to keep our brains healthy and active?

🔊 **10.6**

Claire: First of all, there are many ways in which you can keep your brain working. Many people like to solve sudoku, or crossword puzzles.

Ella: But I hate puzzles. What advice do you have for people like me who don't like them?

Claire: If I were you, I would read. Reading provides excellent exercise for your brain. Whatever you do, don't spend hours watching TV or playing mindless video games. Of course, if you have to play video games, choose games that require you to think and make decisions. In fact, there are games that require players to solve puzzles and problems. Overall, if you like to play games, make sure you choose ones that are good for your brain.

Ella: I know that many students don't have time to eat breakfast in the morning. What's your advice about that?

Claire: Studies show that breakfast is a very important meal because it allows your brain to work efficiently. Make sure that you eat at least one piece of fruit before you leave home in the morning. A good breakfast should contain proteins and grains, like whole-wheat bread. I would also advise you to eat foods that are beneficial for your brain like, berries, nuts, and seeds. These foods help to protect your brain from diseases. It would be a good idea to include these foods in your everyday diet.

Ella: Many people say that chocolate is good for your brain. Should we eat more chocolate?

Claire: It might be good to eat *some* chocolate, but make sure it's dark chocolate not just a normal milk chocolate bar. Dark chocolate helps to stimulate your brain. In fact, a recent study revealed a relationship between the consumption of dark chocolate and winning a Nobel Prize! All in all, you need to learn about foods that are good for your brain.

Ella: What should we do when we feel tired?

Claire: That's simple. You should get enough sleep. It is a well-known fact that, in order to function well, your brain needs rest. People who don't get enough sleep cause car accidents, have problems concentrating, and fall asleep during lectures.

Ella: How many hours should we sleep at night?

Claire: That's a good question. Unfortunately, there's no magic number. The number of hours that you need for your brain to rest will differ from person to person, and will depend on your age and personal needs. Some students need seven hours, while others need nine. However, you ought to sleep around eight hours.

Ella: What else should we do to keep our minds healthy?

Claire: My final advice would be to get plenty of exercise. There's evidence that physical activity has a beneficial effect on your brain. Doing physical exercises increases your thinking skills and your brain volume. It also promotes blood flow and oxygen levels in your brain which stimulates brain function.

Ella: But I don't have time to do any exercises! I have so many assignments!

Claire: If I were you, I'd plan to do simple exercises like walking or jogging every day. So when you have an important assignment or are studying for the exams, don't sit in front of your books for hours.

Ella: OK, well thank you for all your advice. So, to sum up, you said we should be mentally active, eat food that stimulates brain activity, sleep well, and do plenty of exercise. Is that right?

Claire: That sounds about right.

ACKNOWLEDGEMENTS

Author acknowledgements

I would like to give special thanks to all the Cambridge University Press editors for their continuous encouragement and comments. Many thanks go to my colleagues, Claudia Kiburz, Julie Rose, and Christine Thorne for their creativity and enthusiasm for teaching. Finally, I would like to thank my husband, Robert Ryan, for his endless support.
Sabina Ostrowska

Publisher acknowledgements

The publishers are extremely grateful to the following people and their students for reviewing and trialling this course during its development. The course has benefited hugely from your insightful comments and feedback.

Mr M.K. Adjibade, King Saud University, Saudi Arabia; Canan Aktug, Bursa Technical University, Turkey; Olwyn Alexander, Heriot Watt University, UK; Valerie Anisy, Damman University, Saudi Arabia; Anwar Al-Fetlawi, University of Sharjah, UAE; Laila Al-Qadhi, Kuwait University, Kuwait; Tahani Al-Taha, University of Dubai, UAE; Ozlem Atalay, Middle East Technical University, Turkey; Seda Merter Ataygul, Bursa Technical University Turkey; Harika Altug, Bogazici University, Turkey; Kwab Asare, University of Westminster, UK; Erdogan Bada, Cukurova University, Turkey; Cem Balcikanli, Gazi University, Turkey; Gaye Bayri, Anadolu University, Turkey; Meher Ben Lakhdar, Sohar University, Oman; Emma Biss, Girne American University, UK; Dogan Bulut, Meliksah University, Turkey; Sinem Bur, TED University, Turkey; Alison Chisholm, University of Sussex, UK; Dr. Panidnad Chulerk , Rangsit University, Thailand; Sedat Cilingir, Bilgi University, Istanbul, Turkey; Sarah Clark, Nottingham Trent International College, UK; Elaine Cockerham, Higher College of Technology, Muscat, Oman; Asli Derin, Bilgi University, Turkey; Steven Douglass, University of Sunderland, UK; Jacqueline Einer, Sabanci University, Turkey; Basak Erel, Anadolu University, Turkey; Hande Lena Erol, Piri Reis Maritime University, Turkey; Gulseren Eyuboglu, Ozyegin University, Turkey; Muge Gencer, Kemerburgaz University, Turkey; Dr. Majid Gharawi and colleagues at the English Language Centre, Jazan University, Saudi Arabia; Jeff Gibbons, King Fahed University of Petroleum and Minerals, Saudi Arabia; Maxine Gilway, Bristol University UK; Dr Christina Gitsaki, HCT, Dubai Men's College, UAE; Sam Fenwick, Sohar University, Oman; Peter Frey, International House, Doha, Qatar; Neil Harris, Swansea University, UK; Vicki Hayden, College of the North Atlantic, Qatar; Ajarn Naratip Sharp Jindapitak, Prince of Songkla University, Hatyai, Thailand; Joud Jabri-Pickett, United Arab Emirates University, Al Ain, UAE; Aysel Kilic, Anadolu University, Turkey; Ali Kimav, Anadolu University, Turkey; Bahar Kiziltunali, Izmir University of Economics, Turkey; Kamil Koc, Ozel Kasimoglu Coskun Lisesi, Turkey; Ipek Korman-Tezcan, Yeditepe University, Turkey; Philip Lodge, Dubai Men's College, UAE; Iain Mackie, Al Rowdah University, Abu Dhabi, UAE; Katherine Mansfield, University of Westminster, UK; Kassim Mastan, King Saud University, Saudi Arabia; Elspeth McConnell, Newham College, UK; Lauriel Mehdi, American University of Sharjah, UAE; Dorando Mirkin-Dick, Bell International Institute, UK; Dr Sita Musigrungsi, Prince of Songkla University, Hatyai, Thailand; Mark Neville, Al Hosn University, Abu Dhabi, UAE; Shirley Norton, London School of English, UK; James Openshaw, British Study Centres, UK; Hale Ottolini, Mugla Sitki Kocman University, Turkey; David Palmer, University of Dubai, UAE; Michael Pazinas, United Arab Emirates University, UAE; Troy Priest, Zayed University, UAE; Alison Ramage Patterson, Jeddah, Saudi Arabia; Paul Rogers, Qatar Skills Academy, Qatar; Josh Round, Saint George International, UK; Harika Saglicak, Bogazici University, Turkey; Asli Saracoglu, Isik University, Turkey; Neil Sarkar, Ealing, Hammersmith and West London College, UK; Nancy Shepherd, Bahrain University, Bahrain; Jonathan Smith, Sabanci University, Turkey; Peter Smith, United Arab Emirates University, UAE; Adem Soruc, Fatih University Istanbul, Turkey; Dr Peter Stanfield, HCT, Madinat Zayed & Ruwais Colleges, UAE; Maria Agata Szczerbik, United Arab Emirates University, Al Ain, UAE; Burcu Tezcan-Unal, Bilgi University, Turkey; Dr Nakonthep Tipayasuparat, Rangsit University, Thailand; Scott Thornbury, The New School, New York, USA; Susan Toth, HCT, Dubai Men's Campus, Dubai, UAE; Melin Unal, Ege University, Izmir, Turkey; Aylin Unaldi, Bogaziçi University, Turkey; Colleen Wackrow, Princess Nourah bint Abdulrahman University, Riyadh, Saudi Arabia; Gordon Watts, Study Group, Brighton UK; Po Leng Wendelkin, INTO at University of East Anglia, UK; Halime Yildiz, Bilkent University, Ankara, Turkey; Ferhat Yilmaz, Kahramanmaras Sutcu Imam University, Turkey.

Special thanks to Peter Lucantoni for sharing his expertise, both pedagogical and cultural.

Text and Photo acknowledgements

The authors and publishers acknowledge the following sources of copyright material and are grateful for the permissions granted. While every effort has been made, it has not always been possible to identify the sources of all the material used, or to trace all copyright holders. If any omissions are brought to our notice, we will be happy to include the appropriate acknowledgements on reprinting.

p.12:(1) © Eric Limon/Shutterstock; p.12: (2) © szefai/Shutterstock; p.12: (3) © Steven Vidler/Eurasia Press/Corbis; pp.14/15: © Ocean/Corbis; p.25: © Christophe Boisvieux/Corbis; p.27: © Alex Segre/Alamy; pp.32/33: © Dallas & John Heaton/Corbis; pp.50/51: © Tips Images/Tips Italia/Alamy; p.54(a): © Ocean/Corbis; p.54(b): Corbis; p.54(c): © Richard Nowitz/Getty; p.54(d): © Waj/Shutterstock; p.54(e): © Chameleons Eye/Shutterstock; p.59(TR): Turkish School/Getty; p.59(BR): © VladJ55/Shutterstock; p.62: © Mary Evans Picture Library; pp.68/69: © Medio Images/Getty; p.73: © David R Frazier Photo Library/Alamy; p.75: iStockphoto/Thinkstock; p.79: © Global Warming Images/Rex Features; p.86/87: © Michael Melford/NGS/Corbis; p.91: iStockphoto; p.94: © Pascal Deloche/Getty; p.95: AFP/Getty; p.97: © Peteri/Shutterstock; p.99(i): © Eurobanks/Shutterstock; p.99(ii): © Aastock/Shutterstock; p.99(iii): © Asia Images Group Ltd/Alamy; p.99(iv): © Robin Skjoldborg/Getty; pp.104/105: © Frans Lemmens/Alamy; p.108(CL): © Alex Segre/Alamy; p.108(CR): Image Source/Getty; p.108(BL,BR): Image Source/Rex Features; p.112(BR): © Sea Wave/Shutterstock; p.112(BL): © Nenov Brothers Images/Shutterstock; p.113(BR): Stockbyte/Getty; p.113(BL): © Mark Scott/Getty; p.115(TL): © Krzysztof Slusarczyk/Shutterstock; p.115(TR): © Martin Shields/Alamy; p.115(BL): © Jeffery Coolidge/Getty; p.115(BR): © Hera Food/Alamy; p.117: © Mart of Images/Alamy, p.119(T): © John Freeman/Getty; p.119(B): Amand Images/Shutterstock; pp.122/123: © Steven Vidler/Corbis; p.127(TL): © Dave King/Getty; p.127(TR): © Sergey Goruppa/Shutterstock; p.127(CL): © Mike Flippo/Shutterstock; p.127(CR): © Nataliya Hora/Shutterstock; p.129(a): © Triff/Shutterstock; p.129(b): © Tischenko Irina/Shutterstock; p.129(c): © View Stock/Alamy; p.132: Thinkstock; p.135(TL,TR,CL): Thinkstock, p.135(CR): © Horiyan/Shutterstock; p.136: © Vitaly Korovin/Shutterstock; pp.140/141: © Paolo Pellegrin/Magnum Photo Library; p.142 (2) © Stanjoman/Shutterstock; p.142 (3) © David Brabyn/Corbis; p.145: Philips Electrical; p.151: AFP/Getty; p.155: © Alison Wright/Corbis; p.158/159: © Bloomberg/Getty; p.163: © Kushch Dmitry/Alamy; p.165: © Lane Oatey/Getty; pp.176/177: © Sebastian Kaslitzki/Shutterstock; p.181(TL,TR): © DeAgnosti/Getty; p.181(CL): Getty; p.181(CR): © Mondadori/Getty; p.186(sudoko): Thinkstock; p.186 (fruit): © Suslik1983/Shutterstock; p.186(asleep): © Pamplemousse/Getty; p.186(jogging): © Mike Harrington/Digital Vision/Getty.

Videos stills by kind permission of © Discovery Communications LLC 2014

Illustrations

Clive Goodyer p 23; Fiona Gowen pp 91, 98 (top); Ben Hasler (NB Illustration) pp 36, 81; Oxford Designers & Illustrators pp 41, 98 (bottom), 188; Martin Sanders (Beehive Illustration) pp 59, 62

Dictionary

Cambridge dictionaries are the world's most widely used dictionaries for learners of English. Available at three levels (Cambridge Essential English Dictionary, Cambridge Learner's Dictionary and Cambridge Advanced Learner's Dictionary), they provide easy-to-understand definitions, example sentences, and help in avoiding typical mistakes. The dictionaries are also available online at dictionary.cambridge.org. © Cambridge University Press, reproduced with permission.

Corpus

Development of this publication has made use of the Cambridge English Corpus (CEC). The CEC is a multi-billion word computer database of contemporary spoken and written English. It includes British English, American English and other varieties of English. It also includes the Cambridge Learner Corpus, developed in collaboration with Cambridge English Language Assessment. Cambridge University Press has built up the CEC to provide evidence about language use that helps to produce better language teaching materials.

Picture research by Alison Prior.

Typeset by emc design ltd.